1775
Alexander Henry, the Elder explores the Northwest.

Second Spanish expedition under Bodega y Quadra lands on Pacific Coast.

Revolution breaks out in the American colonies.

Outbreak of smallpox strikes colonists in Nova Scotia

Over 300 die as severe storms hit Newfoundland.

William Black, father of N.S. Methodism, arrives in Amherst.

Americans invade Canada, capture Montreal and lay seige to Quebec.

1776
American forces retreat from Quebec after arrival of British reinforcements.

U.S. colonial leaders draft the Declaration of Independence.

Population of Halifax doubles with influx of first Loyalists.

1777
Iroquois of the Six Nations ally with the British.

Burgoyne invades New York capturing Fort Ticonderoga but is forced to surrender at Saratoga.

1778
James Cook lands at Nootka Sound – first Englishman to set foot on Pacific Coast.

France allies with U.S. against Britain.

Butler's Raiders attack U.S. troops and settlements in N.Y. and Ohio Territory.

Frederick Haldimand replaces Guy Carleton as governor of Quebec.

1779
First library is opened at Quebec.

1780

First Loyalist refugees settle in the Niagara Peninsula.

The *Ontario* sinks on Lake Ontario with 30 people lost.

1781
Loyalist John Howe publishes the Halifax *Journal*.

Cornwallis surrenders to Washington at Yorktown, Pennsylvania.

1782
American privateers raid settlement on Atlantic, Bay of Fundy and Gulf of St. Lawrence.

1783
First Loyalists establish Parrtown (Saint John), N.B.

Britain recognizes U.S. claims to lands south of the Great Lakes by Treaty of Versailles.

Royal Montreal Golf Club established – first on continent.

The North West Company formed by merger of Montreal fur trading companies.

1784
Thomas Carleton appointed first governor of New Brunswick.

1785
The power loom is invented.

New Brunswick holds first public elections.

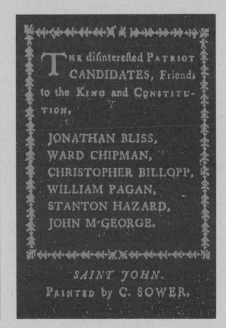

Montreal Gazette and *New Brunswick Royal Gazette* published.

1788
Severe winter, drought and crop failures characterize this as "the Hungry Year."

Bishop Inglis founds King's College at Windsor, N.S.

John Meares constructs first trading post at Friendly Cove on land bought from Nootka chief Maquinna.

Regular sailing packet service established between England and Halifax.

1789
Alexander Mackenzie reaches the Arctic Ocean.

Quebec Turf Club organized.

First Episcopal Conference of Protestant churches held at Quebec.

Redcoats and Loyalists

BRITISH VALOUR and YANKEE BOASTING or, Shannon versus Chesapeake.

*British soldiers drill on the parade square in front of Quebec City's Recollect Friars' Church (left) and the Jesuit Cathedral, gutted by artillery in 1759.
In the post-war period, the presence of the victorious Redcoats everywhere on Quebec streets aggravated the new government's problem of dispensing justice.*

Previous page: *British sailors from aboard the* HMS Shannon *storm aboard the American frigate* Chesapeake *during the blockade of Boston on June 1, 1813.*

Leslie Hannon
Redcoats and Loyalists
1760/1815

Canada's Illustrated Heritage

Canada's Illustrated Heritage

Publisher: Jack McClelland
Editorial Consultant: Pierre Berton
Historical Consultant: Michael Bliss
Editor-in-Chief: Toivo Kiil
Associate Editors: Michael Clugston
Clare McKeon
Harold Quinn
Jean Stinson
Assistant Editor: Marta Howard
Design: William Hindle
Lynn Campbell
Neil Fraser Cochrane
Cover Artist: Alan Daniel
Picture Research: Lembi Buchanan
Michel Doyon
Betty Gibson
Christine Jensen
Margot Sainsbury

ISBN: 0-9196-4415-5

N.S.L. Natural Science of Canada Limited
254 Bartley Drive
Toronto, Ontario M4A 1G1

Printed and bound in Canada

LIEU\.^t GEN\.^l SIR GEORGE PROVOST
GOVERNOR OF CANADA.

Sir George, who twice managed to pluck humiliation from the jaws of victory, is lampooned (and his name, Prevost, misspelled) by a sharp-quilled illustrator. At the battle of Sackett's Harbour in 1813, Prevost withdrew at the moment his victory seemed assured. At Plattsburg the following year, his ineptness forced retreat. He died a week before his court martial.

Contents

Water wagons and traders go about their business in Quebec City after the war's end. Wolfe's artillery, mounted across the St. Lawrence at Point-Lévis, had poked holes in the Bishop's House and destroyed nearby buildings. British ships command the harbour, as the city learns to live under a new flag.

6

Conflicts of Loyalty

May the unanimity among all classes of citizens cause all distinctions and prejudices to disappear, make the country flourish, and render it always happy.

Drinking toast, Quebec, 1791

In British North America, it was a time of war and peace, then of war again. From the Plains of Abraham to Queenston Heights, Canada became a northern bastion for all the King's men. In the outside world, it was the era that ended at the battle of Waterloo.

That's how it was recorded by the ruling classes, the military, the merchants and the bureaucrats – few outside that circle could read or write. To the average man or woman, the great majority of Canada's six hundred thousand people, it was a time of conflicting loyalties that split brother from brother, of racial tension, of martial law, of burned and pillaged homesteads, of hungry children, and, as always, of unremitting back-breaking work. The people's war was primarily against the forest, the winter and the silent vastness of space.

In the first half-century of British rule, the northern colonies from the Atlantic to the Great Lakes – most of the huge territory still primeval wilderness – were almost continually shaken by conflict, from within and without. Yet, stubbornly, more ground was cleared and broken each season,

the fringe of settlement widened, trade struggled and strenghtened, and those few with time and taste introduced some of the arts.

As memories of the Conquest faded, and surprisingly sympathetic governors sat in the Château St. Louis at Quebec, a sharing and a collaboration between French and English began, slowly, even grudgingly, but definitely. It found a sure expression in the mutual determination to deny the northlands to godless republicanism. French as well as English fought for this country.

There were even some visionaries who began to dream about a new and separate nation above the Great Lakes. But William Pitt, prime minister of Great Britain, was closer to the general sentiment when he mused: "Some are for keeping Canada, some Guadeloupe. Who will tell me which I shall be hanged for not keeping?" To most of the world, Canada was as little known as the backside of the moon.

Although the period is dominated by its military and political figures – and our knowledge is mostly drawn from their journals or official reports – the record provides us with quite ordinary personalities who, in their independence, loyalty and determination provided Canada with the human stuff that eventually nourished a nation.

Such a man was John Walten Meyers. His bones lie today on a glacial ridge between the eastern Ontario cities of Belleville and Trenton along

Wednesday night an amicable society of journeymen taylors met at a flate-houfe in the neighbourhood of Weftminfter, but being foon intoxicated with drinking healths to the fafe arrival of her intended Majefty, they fell to loggerheads about the difpofal of our late conquefts in North America, when one of the Members unfortunately moving, that Canada fhould be given up for the retention of Guadaloupe, he had his head broke with a gallon pot, and was kicked out of company.

The London Chronicle in 1761 gave this report of an argument over whether England should keep Canada. One man was bashed for suggesting that it be returned to France in exchange for the isle of Guadeloupe.

The conquest of Canada merely shelved for a time Britain's rivalry with France and other European neighbours. The Political Register *lampooned Parliament in 1769 for doting on petty domestic affairs (below) while Frederick the Great of Prussia, Maria Theresa of Austria, Louis XV of France and Charles II of Spain plotted the partition of the British Empire.*

the Bay of Quinte. In 1816 Belleville was given the affectionate nickname of Arabella Gore, wife of the lieutenant-governor of Upper Canada, but long before the turn of the 19th century it was known as Meyers' Creek.

John Meyers was born on January 22, 1745, in Albany County, New York. His Prussian father had emigrated to the American colonies, carving out a farm near Poughkeepsie. The family prospered and John married Polly Kruger, from another immigrant family. When rebellion flamed, thousands of colonial families were split in their loyalties. So it was on the Meyers' homestead: John declared for the King; his father for the Republic.

The rebels were in a local majority and there was muttering after Bunker Hill about John being a British spy. His mother warned him to flee, offering to take care of Polly and their children. With a much loved old dog, John set out on foot for Canada.

Skirting all settlements, splashing through swamps, both master and animal became exhausted and faint from hunger. When the dog could go no further, John carried him. Humane? Well, yes, but the fugitive later admitted he also reckoned on the animal as a last-ditch meal. A friendly Mohawk lifted the famine with a gift of bear meat.

Enlisting in Quebec, John took part in "Gentleman Johnny" Burgoyne's ill-fated campaign in 1777 into the Hudson Valley. Later, he was promoted captain by Governor-General Frederick Haldimand and given a company in Edward Jessup's Loyal Rangers. When the Revolution ended, all Loyalists were offered land grants in the remaining British territories and John Meyers drew a forest lot in the Ninth Township (Hastings County).

A few years later, seeking a site where he could build a flour mill, he purchased, for twenty pounds, land on the banks of a river rushing into the Bay of Quinte. The river was soon known as Meyers' Creek (later the Moira). Meyers' mill was grinding by 1790, when the site of Toronto was inhabited only by ducks.

Meyers the Tory, the monarchist, was one of the fifty thousand Loyalists who fled north into Canada and the Maritimes, changing the French-English balance of the country forever. But he was typical, too, in his business endeavour, his urge to succeed. He believed in work and the notion that a man could make something of himself.

It didn't simply mean to get rich by any road. When Thomas Jefferson – no more American than John Meyers – wrote about "the pursuit of happiness" he had these workaday aims in mind. John Meyers and his fellows dyed them indissolubly into the Canadian fabric.

By 1794, John was living in one of the two brick houses in what is now Ontario (the other was the Baby homestead on the Detroit shore). The bricks were baked from clay dug on Meyers' own property in Sidney Township. Joined by Polly and his four sons, John became a frequent and generous host to all dignitaries passing along the Quinte from Kingston to Cobourg and York.

Like many of his contemporaries, Meyers kept several Negro slaves. One of them, known as Black Bet, was so devoted to the family that when freed by law she refused to leave the household.

In the earliest pioneer years in a roadless province, people and their goods were moved by *bateaux,* sturdy flat-bottomed boats, along the shorelines of the lakes. As he prospered, John Meyers branched out into transport, carrying sawn lumber and grain to Kingston, even down the St. Lawrence to Montreal.

If freight was consigned John usually carried passengers for free. The record shows that he was always well supplied at home or afloat with British "grog" (rum from the West Indies), and that he had a liberal hand at the spigot.

Before he died, at the respectable age of seventy-six, Captain John had seen his chosen Canada repeatedly reject and repel the advances of his American kin, pierce the western mountains to the Pacific, reach and map the Arctic frontier, bring a humming life to the clearings in the eastern forest and begin to farm the rich earth of the prairies. His life was in itself the story of those years.

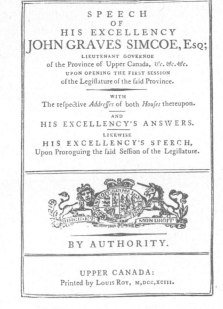

John Graves Simcoe had seen duty in the American Revolutionary War, had commanded the Queen's Rangers, and was a member of the British House of Commons when he was appointed the first lieutenant-governor of Upper Canada in 1791. He arrived the next year to open the legislature at Niagara-on-the-Lake, which he renamed Newark. Then, in 1793, he moved the capital to Toronto Bay, renaming it York.

Any map of the "inhabited" portion of Canada in 1777 would encompass little – the white population was 90,000. However, as the scene on the frontispiece of this French survey suggests, the fur trade had already extended into the remote interior.

9

Cutters, sleighs and carts drawn by horses and oxen, and small sleighs pulled by dogs, dot the snow-covered shoreline of the St. Charles River in the north-west part of Quebec City. Bundled against winter's chill, sightseers and workers glide below a skyline dominated by the church spires of the fortified city.

CHAPTER ONE

Under the New Flag

*At Montreal the Civilians & Military
are Inveterate Enemies, I am ashamed to
say, from the most trifling Circumstances.*

Governor James Murray, 1764

At nine o'clock on the evening of Thursday, December 6, 1764, the wealthy Montreal fur trader Thomas Walker, his wife and two friends were lingering over supper. The three household servants refilled glasses and bustled between table and kitchen as the ebullient Walker, a recently appointed magistrate, held forth on his favorite subject: the arrogance of the officers of the British garrison. No one heard the crunch of boots on packed snow as a platoon of about twenty men appeared in the moonlit street.

Without warning, the door flew open and six masked men stormed inside. As Mrs. Walker screamed and ran from the room with the guests, the intruders knocked the judge senseless. A blade flashed in the lamplight and one of Walker's ears was lopped. Carrying the grisly trophy, the attackers vanished. A short while later, at the headquarters of the 28th Regiment, the door to the adjutant's office was opened just enough to permit a small package to be tossed onto the desk. It contained the ear.

The hullabaloo that followed turned Montreal into an armed camp; townsfolk carried weapons in the streets and some shopkeepers conducted business with loaded pistols on their counters. Britain's new colony of Canada seethed with unrest. Governor James Murray, hurrying to Montreal from Quebec City, said it almost seemed as though two hostile armies were about to collide. Reverberations shook the Altantic cities of Boston and New York, and when the news reached London, the government offered a reward of one hundred guineas to anyone who would turn in the culprits. Judge Walker himself offered another hundred guineas and the other merchants of Montreal put up £300 sterling. A group of officers, including the famous Saint-Luc de la Corne, were arrested but all were acquitted.

The severing of an ear, or any permanent marking of a man, was the deepest of insults. Britain had actually declared war against Spain earlier in the century after Captain Robert Jenkins had an ear sliced off by a Spaniard who boarded his brig off Cuba. The affair of Walker's ear did not have such a sensational aftermath but it brought to wide attention the curious and explosive situation that had arisen along the St. Lawrence Valley.

Although Montreal – and with it the rest of New France – had been surrendered in the autumn of 1760, more than three years passed before the Treaty of Paris set out the formal terms of the capitulation. Young King George III was now on the throne (he was so ignorant of North America that he confused India's Ganges with the Ohio River)

Seals bearing coats of arms and mottos, like Gov. James Murray's "Deum Time," were impressions in melted wax used to authenticate documents or signify office. They were also used to close letters: a seal discouraged the curious and a broken seal betrayed uninvited eyes.

James Murray
Quebec's British Governor

For three years after the French surrender, Quebeckers lived under martial law, and the task of ruling the "old and new subjects" fell to James Murray. A military man, he had seen action at Louisbourg and Quebec, but unlike most others in the army's top brass, he advocated a policy of leniency and compromise in dealing with the French-speaking majority. His fiercest opponents were the English merchants — "that group of Licentious Fanaticks," he called them — who had flooded into the province after the war, hoping to reap the spoils of conquest. In 1766, they forced London to recall Murray, to face charges of misrule, but he was acquitted. He never returned to Canada, and spent part of his later years as governor of the Mediterranean island of Minorca.

and his cabinet seriously debated simply returning the conquered lands to the French.

The territories then known as Canada were widely considered to be of doubtful value. Britain was already established on the Atlantic seaboard all the way from Florida to Newfoundland, and the Royal Navy controlled the oceans. The Hudson's Bay Company from its private realm would ensure the supply of furs – the only visible trading asset of the inhospitable north. If a choice was to be made of captured French territory, why not give back rocky Canada and retain the sunny territory of Guadeloupe? The traders pointed out that the West Indian island group had a much larger population than did New France and would, at a stroke, provide sugar, rum, cotton and coffee.

social courtesies, hangmen's ropes

It took the combined influence of William Pitt, builder of the British Empire, and Benjamin Franklin, architect of the American nation, then resident in London, to ensure that the Crown held on to the conquests of Wolfe and Amherst. The aging Pitt refused the post of governor of Canada (salary: £5,000 a year), and General James Murray, who had been military governor of Quebec since the battle on the Plains of Abraham, was appointed to the larger civil responsibility.

Right from the start, the British administrators realized their forces were but a handful amid the total *Canadien* population of perhaps eighty thousand, spread from the Gaspé to New Orleans, and they acted accordingly. Murray insisted that the social courtesies be observed, and with the hangman's rope he stopped looting. The Redcoat officers got along very well with the educated Roman Catholic priests and landowning *seigneurs* who, as a class, came nearest to resembling the landed aristocracy of England.

It was a very different story between the British military and the traders, fortune hunters and discharged servicemen who first drifted, then swarmed into Quebec, Trois Rivières and Montreal after Wolfe's victory. Without competitors, they simply took over the great bulk of the colony's commerce and many quickly grew rich.

old subjects, new subjects

These merchants and any other English-speaking "old subjects" had been specifically invited to make their homes in Canada – now officially "the Province of Quebec." They had been promised all the blessings of the British way of life, and eventually, a representative assembly drawn from the property owners of the province. The authorities in fact hoped to attract enough English settlers to act as a counterweight to the mass of French-speaking "new subjects." With similar intent, a scheme was mooted to replace the Church of Rome with the Church of England.

As soon as civil government became a fact on August 10, 1764, the merchant group – most of them from the American seaboard colonies – began to agitate for an assembly. They numbered only about four hundred and fifty and their most outspoken leader was Thomas Walker.

It was still a time of extreme class differences, both in Europe and in the colonies. The feudal system was a long time a'dying, and the American and French revolutions were still a decade in the future. Naval and army officers were drawn almost exclusively from the upper classes. The British officer caste in North America despised those in trade, and were at first astonished and then enraged when "money-grubbing shopkeepers" dared to push their claims for democratic rights. The 18th-century man-in-the-street was lucky to have the bare rudiments of learning. His life was harsh and short, and although England's Bill of Rights was nearly a century old, its fine principles had yet to take on any real substance for most common people.

Governor Murray had to make some attempt to obey ill-conceived instructions received from London. Ordered to establish a system of justice "as near as may be agreeable to the laws of England," Murray set up courts and police, with regular trials in Quebec and Montreal. No Roman Catholic could hold an official appointment, and magistrates were appointed only from among the "old subjects"–among them the intractable Thomas Walker.

On his own responsibility, Murray ordered that in the Court of King's Bench (where serious cases were tried) jurors were to be drawn from "all His Majesty's Subjects in this Colony, without Distinction." In the Court of Common Pleas (the lower court) he allowed the *advocats* among the "new subjects" to appear for clients. He interpreted his instructions to allow the *Canadiens* to retain their own civil laws, particularly those relating to land. The "Johnny-come-lately" merchants were furious.

explosive stand-off

On the vital question of an elected assembly, Murray (like his successors for many years) would not budge an inch. Only Protestants owning land freehold in the English tradition (principally the trader group) would be qualified for election. Thus the tenant-farming *habitants* (numbering over seventy thousand in the St. Lawrence Valley) would be without voice or power.

Not only was this prospect repugnant to any sense of justice or fairness, but it would almost certainly foment strife–and the *Canadiens* had proved themselves tough guerrilla fighters in a hundred years of wilderness campaigns.

The explosive stand-off between the governor's

A bilingual advertising supplement in the Quebec Gazette of August 2, 1764, offered a variety of good buys including fine imported liquors; a "parcel" of beaver, bear and raccoon furs; a house, stable and two-thirds of the island of St. Paul, belonging to the French East-India Co.; and a reward for a run-away servant girl – rather short and "inclined to Fat."

Aaron Hart, Merchant

Coincidentally, two of the first Jewish families to settle in Canada were named Hart: Samuel Hart and his three brothers who arrived in Halifax in 1751, and Aaron Hart (no relation), a British army officer who served under Jeffrey Amherst at Montreal and settled in Trois Rivières after the war. The latter Hart quickly built a thriving business from the fur trade, operated numerous other enterprises in the town, and acquired vast tracts of seigneurial lands. Before his death in 1800, he had sired eleven children, established the commercial foundation of Trois Rivières, and become one of the richest men in the country.

THE CONDITION of this Recognizance is such, That whereas the above named *Aaron Hart* ——— is licenced to keep a common Ale-house, or Victualling-house, for one whole Year, to be computed from the Twenty-fifth Day of *March last* in the House *he* now dwelleth, at *Three Rivers in the District* aforesaid; if *he* the said *Aaron Hart* ——— shall keep and maintain good Order and Rule, and shall suffer no Disorders, or unlawful Games to be used in *his* said House, or in any Out-house, Yard, Garden, or Back-side thereunto belonging, during the said Term, then this Recognizance to be void, otherwise to remain in full Force.

Isaac Levy
John Franks
William Laing

Taken and acknowledged } before me

Geo. Allsopp
D.Ect

Hart was granted a "common Ale-house" licence in 1768, valid if he allowed no disorders.

party, the *seigneurs* and the priests on one side, and the British-American merchants, their employees and influential commercial connections in London on the other, lasted throughout the early decades of British rule in Canada. If the lid never quite blew off, there were almost continuous eruptions.

Using their new powers, the magistrates hit back at the hated military by sentencing prankish soldiers to severe sentences. Judge Walker enraged the officers by ruling against them whenever possible, particularly in billeting matters, and it was following a billeting dispute that Walker lost his ear.

atheists, infidels and even Jews

It was a brutal and vengeful act but it symbolized many deep-running social, class and political problems. The victors were, in essence, fighting among themselves. Petitions from both sides were carried across the Atlantic by the tall ships every summer. Although the trader faction soon got Governor Murray recalled, his replacements followed basically the same policies.

Murray's dislike of commerce was obsessive, blinding him to the fact that there were men of good character and goodwill among those to whom he referred as "the Licentious Fanaticks." He also labelled them "Quakers, Puritans, Anabaptists, Presbyterians, Atheists, Infidels and even Jews." When a grand jury composed mostly of the "old subjects" had the nerve to lecture the governor about how the colony should be ruled, Murray threatened to expel them from Quebec. "The genteel people of this country despise merchants and, of course, esteem the officers who shun them most."

Many of the traders had brought with them from the Thirteen Colonies an equal hatred of the supercilious Redcoat officers. They hired an agent in England to plead their case to the King. Murray, they wrote, frequently treated them "with a Rage and Rudeness of Language and Demeanour, as dishonorable to the Trust he holds as painful to those who suffer from it."

They asked for a new governor "acquainted with other maxims of Government than Military only," and got their new governor in 1766 – Colonel Guy Carleton, a gentleman from Ulster, another of Wolfe's officers. They were soon quarreling just as bitterly with the austere Carleton as they had with the passionate Murray.

All the early British rulers of Canada openly admired the French Canadian way of life, particularly that of the *seigneurs,* those backwoods lords of Quebec manors who ruled with concern and firmness over their many thousands of tenant small-holders. The mass of the peasantry – pious, well-fed, secure in their own snug homes – asked for nothing more, and offered respect and obedience to their *petite noblesse.*

Before the end of the French regime, virtually all the land on both sides of the St. Lawrence, from the Gaspé to above Montreal, had been parcelled into two hundred and fifty seigneuries – large estates granted by the French Crown to well-connected persons or institutions.

parcelling the land

Under the colonizing energy of Cardinal Richelieu, the *seigneurs* had been charged with the duty of creating fertile farms. From their large tracts they were obliged to grant farm-lots to emigrant peasants, soon to be known as *habitants.* When Louis XIV took personal charge of New France, he decided that many of the *seigneurs* were merely land speculators and he confiscated those grants, placing the whole land-tenure system directly under the control of the governor's first minister, the *intendant.*

This powerful bureaucrat ensured that the tenant-farmers, the *censitaires,* were not exploited. They were never serfs; in fact, some European observers noted that the *habitants* in Canada lived in greater comfort than did most of the gentry in France.

Before arterial roads were built, every man had to have access to the river for transportation and commerce – the canoe in summer and sleigh in winter. The farm lots of the *habitants* were thus almost always long oblongs, perhaps six hundred feet in width, stretching back about a mile from the water.

simple and secure

Outside the urban centres of Quebec, Trois Rivières and Montreal, the great bulk of the population lived in simple homes of whitewashed stone or rough-hewn timber, sometimes a mixture of both. Built in a line paralleling the river, the buildings were low in profile, narrow, the roof projecting its eaves over the walls. Downstairs, there was living room, kitchen and the parent's bedroom, with a lean-to storeroom at the rear.

The relationship between the *habitant* and *seigneur* was normally a simple and easy one. The *habitants* were required to make a yearly gesture of loyalty to the *seigneur,* but their obligations in peacetime were far from onerous. On St. Martin's Day each year they paid a trifling annual fee, known as the *cens,* for their land. This was accompanied by another small tribute, known as the *rentes,* usually consisting of grain, poultry or other produce.

In the rare event of a *censitaire* selling his farm, the *seigneur* could claim a payment, known as the *lods et ventes,* amounting to one-twelfth of the price. If the *seigneur* should sell his own property, the Crown demanded a tax of one-fifth, known as the *quint.*

All able-bodied *habitants* were subject to the

salt	50 *sols* per *minot*
pepper	20 *sols* per *once*
chickens	1 *livre* each
geese	1 *livre* and 5 *sols* each
sheep	15 *livres* each
pigs	22 *livres* each
pewter dishes	15 *sols* each
gun shot	4 *livres* per thousand
nails	20 *livres* per thousand
glass beads	8 *sols* per *livre*
hand saws	18 *livres* 15 *sols* each
winter coats	3 *livres* each
ladies' shoes	100 *sols* each
iron pots	6 *livres* each
scissors	7 *sols* a pair
rosary beads	7 *sols* a string
olive oil	14 *sols* a pot
gun powder	30 *sols* a horn
guns	20 *livres* each

The jumbled currency of early Canada complicated commerce with French livres and sols, Portuguese "Joes," Spanish piastres, British pounds and sterling from Halifax, New England and New York. Goods measured in minots (a peck or two gallons), strings and horns were purchased on yearly salaries, from the governor-general's £2,000 and a schoolmaster's £100, to a clerk's £90 and a chimney sweep's £60.

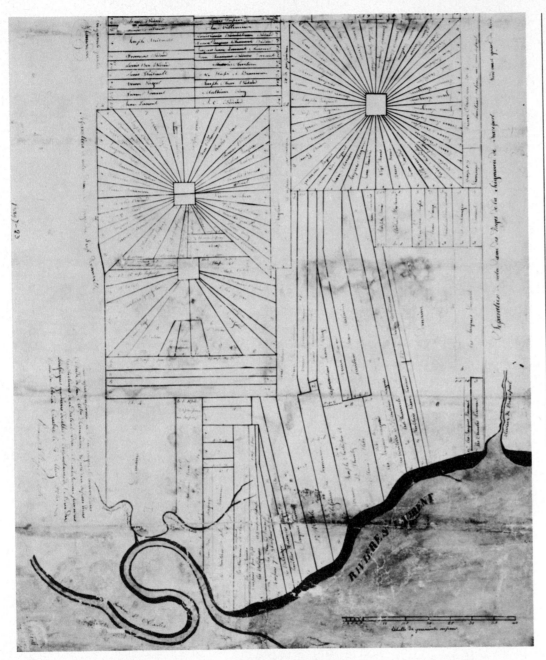

Devised to foster a self-sufficient and stable agricultural society, the seigneurial method of land tenure was a derivative of the feudal system transplanted in Canada in 1623. The map shows the allotment of lands to censitaires *(tenants) in the seigneuries of Charlesbourg and Beauport near Quebec City. The small squares at centre represent the landowners' manors.*

corvée, a yearly contribution of work for no pay. The maximum a *seigneur* could demand was six days per year, but he usually settled for three – one day each at ploughing, seeding and harvesting. There were a few other perks. Only the *seigneur* could have a gristmill and the tenants were obliged to use it, leaving behind one-fourteenth of their flour. Under the *droit de pêche,* the *seigneur* could claim one fish of every eleven caught, and the *droit de coupe de bois* permitted him to cut wood anywhere. He had pride of place at official functions, a free pew in the church and the right to be buried beneath it.

lord of the manor

While the lord of the manor was sometimes little better off financially than his humblest tenants, and sometimes worked as hard, he had very definite duties towards them. Primarily, he had to provide the *manoir habité* – the centre of the settlement – where the new emigrant could seek help and technical advice in the loneliness of the early years, and the protection of numbers in time of Indian attack.

His mill, built of rough stones slitted for musketry, often served as the local strongpoint. He had to maintain at his own expense the court where he sat as judge in minor cases. He was responsible in part for the upkeep of the parish church and for lodging the priest.

On the first of May each year, the winter snows forgotten, the *habitants* arrived at the *manoir* in their best clothes, the youths bearing a tall fir with branches and bark stripped to within a few feet of the tip. This was dug in before the house, and embellished with strings and ribbons. The *seigneur* and his family came out to sit in chairs and applaud as couples kicked up their heels, dancing around the maypole. Flasks of liquor were passed, and fusillades of blank cartridges, hand-packed for

16

the occasion, roared from the bushes.

All were invited into the stone-built *manoir* where food was laid out on long tables. The *seigneur* tapped the brandy cask and the *censitaires* rushed outside to blast away at the fir pole until it was blackened with powder burns.

On these ribbon farms a self-sufficient human enclave had developed over a century-and-a-half. A class of farmers of the Old World had been implanted in the New (then abandoned by corrupt bureaucrats and decadent monarchs), hemmed in by the frozen rivers and the impossible forests. Yet the habitants were fertile: in the ten years after the Union Jack was raised over Quebec, the birthrate reached an amazing 65.2 per 1,000 population. Families of fifteen children were commonplace, and a bachelor was an object of derision.

hooked rugs and homespun

Each habitant house was flanked by barn, stable, the half-buried root-cellar where perishables were stored and the stone bread oven. All trees and brush were cleared away – a precaution against both raids and fire. The winter winds howling off the ridged river ice called for a huge pile of split logs to stoke the fire that burned for months on end in the wide stone fireplace.

The interior revealed gaily coloured hooked rugs on the floors, one or two imported pieces of furniture, perhaps a sideboard storing all the family crockery and cutlery, a set of dining chairs, a spinning wheel to produce yarn for homespun clothing (the *étoffe du pays*), benches, stools and couches made by the farmer and his sons, colourful pictures of the saints on the walls.

Candles were a luxury in the Canadian countryside at the close of the 18th century. A tallow lamp with floating wick provided the light. Most folks got up early, went to bed early. At night, after an ample dinner of *soupe aux pois,* meat or

Habitant Fashion

Habitant clothes of the 18th century were ideally suited to the climate. Below, the woman wears a long cloak, fur muff and an enormous tubular wind-break hat. At right, the man wears homespun trousers and jacket, tied with a blue sash, and the traditional red toque; the woman a blue high-waisted woollen dress and long-visored cap. All wear ankle-length Indian-type moccasins.

Travel in Quebec

Walking and riding horseback were the most common and comfortable ways of travelling the roads of Quebec. Farmers brought their goods to market in wooden carts, and those with money braved the few passable roads in high-wheeled *calèches*. Until 1783, the only "highway" was the rutted Quebec-Montreal road. In summer, barges ferried horses and vehicles across rivers, but with the winter freeze-up, carioles and cutters all took to the ice for quicker and smoother rides.

The coiled springs at the rear of this calèche *slightly reduced the pummeling passengers got.*

The stagecoach at left may well have been one of those that travelled the 24-stage run between Montreal and Quebec. The woodcart (centre) was a familiar sight.

fish, or *tourtière,* wheaten bread and cakes made from finely ground corn, the *habitant* could sit by his fireside, sip his homebrew ale, puff his clay pipe full of *tabac Canadienne,* and consider that if only the great men of Europe would go and fight their battles elsewhere he would be totally content.

A few families had risen to positions of wealth and grandeur. Several had been granted titles – as counts, earls, barons, even one marquis – by the French Crown; and all other *seigneurs* were accorded the monicker, *Sieur* (Sir). One worried intendant had written his King that "pride and sloth are the great faults of the people of Canada . . . I pray you to grant no more letters of nobility." Some of the richest of the *seigneurs* had accepted the British offer of free transportation to France, but the majority stayed.

Barons of Longueuil

When British civil government began along the St. Lawrence, the Le Moynes had been established on their *seigneury* at Longueuil for 117 years. From lowly beginnings (the first Le Moyne was the son of a Dieppe tavern-keeper) they had produced outstanding leaders, in war and peace, including the founder of New Orleans. Their towered château, measuring some two hundred feet in length by one hundred and seventy in breadth, was a famous sight on the shore opposite Montreal. The Le Moyne mill was the finest in the land, their stone-built brewery scented the air for miles, and their spired church was the envy of all. The family had been raised to the dignity of Barons of Longueuil, and this was the only French title in North America to be sustained by the British.

The affinity of the British and French upper crust in Canada was revealed most noticeably when a Le Moyne widow married the Montreal merchant William Grant and, not long afterwards, her daughter married Captain David Grant of the 94th Regiment, nephew of her stepfather.

When the tall, forty-two-year-old bachelor, Guy Carleton succeeded James Murray as governor in 1766, the colony came under the jurisdiction of a firm but fair-minded autocrat. A thrice wounded career soldier, Carleton's first official statement was that he intended to draw no distinctions between the various groups of His Majesty's Canadian subjects, but only between the worthy and the unworthy. He also announced that he was not accepting fees and pay-offs which were a feature of colonial appointments. "There is a certain appearance of dirt, a sort of meaness, in exacting fees on every occasion."

firm Canadian roots

Although both Carleton and the Chief Justice of Quebec, William Hey, had been lobbied before they left England to favour the rights of the "old subjects," they were immediately faced with the realities of Quebec. Soon Carleton was writing home to the Colonial Secretary, Lord Shelburne, pointing out drily that he had under command sixteen hundred troops and that the "old subjects," scattered about the province, numbered only about four hundred. On the other hand, the "new subjects" – that is, the *Canadiens* – could put into the battlefield eighteen thousand well-trained men, accustomed to obey their *seigneurs,* who were also their officers.

It was foolish, Carleton asserted, to believe that British emigration would ever even the scales in Quebec. "So," he concluded, "barring a catastrophe shocking to think of, this country to the end of time must be peopled by the Canadian race who have already taken such firm root that any new stock transplanted will be totally and imperceptibly hid amongst them."

The French could not be Anglicized, but there was some prospect of binding them in loyalty to

Guy Carleton
Architect of Two Canadas

A twenty-year veteran of the army and a friend of General Wolfe, Guy Carleton came to Canada in 1759 and was wounded in battle at the Plains of Abraham. In 1766, he replaced James Murray as governor, inheriting with the post all the problems of governing the province. He spoke French fluently and was the chief spokesman for the cause of *Quebecois* language and religious rights, guaranteed by the Quebec Act in 1774 and the Constitutional Act in 1791. His marriage in 1772 was a gala affair, attended by the cream of Quebec society, English and French, and before his death in 1808, he fathered 11 children. As a military man, his command of Quebec during the American seige kept the beleaguered town strong until reinforcements from abroad forced the Americans to retreat.

"This sir, is the meaning of the Quebec Act!" reads the caption of this 1774 cartoon. In an effort to placate the majority, the Act blended English and French law, confusing many.

the Crown. The chaos resulting from attempts to introduce English common law had to be untangled. The question of the representative assembly had to be faced. The fears that had sparked the uprising of the western Indian tribes under Pontiac and the American intention to push across the Alleghenies . . . all those complex matters had to be resolved.

The solutions, after four years of heated argument, were built into the Quebec Act of 1774, Carleton's master plan, the first constitution of Canada.

While he was in England in 1772 to advise the drafters of the bill, "grave Carleton" (as General James Wolfe had dubbed him), now forty-eight, proposed in turn to the two daughters of the Earl of Effingham. He got a rejection from the older Lady Anne but an eager acceptance from the pretty eighteen-year-old Lady Maria. Anne promptly said yes to Carleton's soldier nephew, who was given an appointment on his uncle's staff. All four were back in Quebec by mid-September, 1774. No, not four, six! Carleton was already the father of two, and the family of this oddly matched pair would eventually reach a total of eleven, nine sons and two daughters. Carleton wasn't all that grave.

While the delightful May-September romance bloomed in the Château St. Louis at Quebec, and as the King's French-speaking subjects expressed their general satisfaction with the new legislation, a violent storm, long threatening, blew up from the south.

The so-called Boston Massacre had ignited the fuse of patriot reaction to British tax enforcement, and the "Boston Tea Party" had brought the kettle of discontent to the boil. The First Continental Congress was in session in Carpenter's Hall, Philadelphia, even as Carleton and his bride stepped off the ship at Wolfe's Cove.

La Gallerie des Modes

Around 1780, fashion news from Europe began to travel with the publication of coloured plates in magazines, and well-to-do Canadians adopted the new mode in costume – the English country style. Gone were the ruffles, lace and embroidery of the French Court of pre-revolution days, and simplicity became the vogue. William Berczy's group portrait of Montreal's Woolsey family (1809) is a stunning record of the new fashion. Mrs. Woolsey wears a high-waisted robe en chemise, similar to the dress of her daughters, under a pink overdress. Her husband and older son sport plain cloth cutaway coats with high collars, contrasting knee breeches tucked into riding boots, and plain neckcloths. Grandmother's austere dress is copied in the child's doll, and the boys wear plain two-piece playsuits.

Thomas Davies' Canada

In their colour, brilliance, clarity and detail, the paintings of Thomas Davies are a complete departure from the topographic watercolours of his Royal Military Academy contemporaries. Davies was posted in Canada between 1755 and 1790, and although his views at times are superbly naïve, they are by far the most stunning record of society and landscape at the time.

Davies portrayed activity typical to rural Quebec of 1790 in his View of the Bridge on the River La Puce, *against a backdrop of autumn splendour.*

"The farm-houses hereabouts," wrote traveller Peter Kalm, "are generally built along the rising banks of the river . . . almost every farmer has a kitchen garden . . . the houses are built of stone, but sometimes of timber . . . the roofs are covered with boards, and the chinks are filled up with clay. Other farm buildings are covered with straw."

With near-photographic precision, Davies rendered this view of the village of Château-Richer, its broad saltmarsh, fishing weirs and habitant *farmbuildings.*

The British Army established this hut camp, protectively dug into the embankments of the Dykman farm, in New York. Between skirmishes with the American militiamen and army, the soldiers cleaned their rifles, paused for a pipe, endured a shave or played cards, while the less fortunate marched off on patrol. Though well-equipped, British soldiers were mainly a sorry lot from slums and jails, commanded by officers who purchased, rather than earned, commissions.

CHAPTER TWO

The Heavy Hand of Uncle Sam

*I cannot but lament ... the impending
Calamities Britain and her Colonies are
about to suffer ... Passion governs and
she never governs wisely ...*

Benjamin Franklin, 1775

The ragtag bunch in the shadows waited for a cloud to mask the face of the moon. Before them across a forest clearing lay Fort Ticonderoga, guardian of Lake Champlain. It was in the early hours of May 10, 1775.

The star-shaped fort at the southern end of the narrow lake bristled with a hundred cannon – more than enough to hold the strategic Hudson-Richelieu waterway against all comers. Two sentries yawned at the wicket gate while the rest of the garrison of forty Redcoats slept in their bunks.

News of the skirmish at Lexington three weeks earlier had no doubt reached Captain William Delaplace, the elderly British commander, but it was discounted as just another flare-up with those damned Yankee agitators. The regular soldier of those times was contemptuous of all amateurs and, in any case, a real shooting war – a civil war within the British family – still seemed unthinkable.

The men in the shadows, passing bottles of whisky from hand to hand, were part of the most unlikely army ever mustered. Dressed in everything from braided uniforms to backwoods homespun under coonskin caps, armed with all manner of muskets, pistols, knives and rusty swords, they were known as the Green Mountain Boys from Vermont.

Ethan Allen, a brawling frontier bully, president of the Onion River Land Company, was their leader. This was, in fact, his clan's private vigilante corps, formed to fight off land speculators from New York and New Hampshire. They turned patriotic overnight when leaders of the infant army of the Thirteen Colonies, now encircling Boston, called urgently for artillery. Could the guns guarding the British fortresses in the Champlain Pass be taken and turned against the King? A further lure was Allen's promise of all the rum his men could drink and all the loot they could carry away.

Allen's second-in-command was thirty-four-year-old Benedict Arnold, a newly promoted colonel in the Massachusetts militia. The brilliant, intransigent Arnold was to play a fascinating role – from wounded hero to despised traitor – as the revolution rolled onward.

When a high-riding cloud suddenly obscured the moon, the eighty Green Mountain Boys dashed forward, whoopin' and hollerin', and stormed the gate. The Americans raced across the parade ground and barred the doors of the barracks, bottling up the garrison. Capt. Delaplace, in his dressing gown, awakened by Allen's roar for surrender, "in the name of the great Jehovah and

TEUCRO DUCE NIL DESPERANDOM.

First Battalion of PENNSYLVANIA LOYALISTS, commanded by His Excellency Sir WILLIAM HOWE, K.B.

ALL INTREPID ABLE-BODIED

HEROES,

WHO are willing to serve His MAJESTY KING GEORGE the Third, in Defence of their Country, Laws and Constitution, against the arbitrary Usurpations of a tyrannical Congress, have now not only an Opportunity of manifesting their Spirit, by assisting in reducing to Obedience their too-long deluded Countrymen, but also of acquiring the polite Accomplishments of a Soldier, by serving only two Years, or during the present Rebellion in America.

Such spirited Fellows, who are willing to engage, will be rewarded at the End of the War, besides their Laurels, with 50 Acres of Land, where every gallant Hero may retire, and enjoy his Bottle and Lass.

Each Volunteer will receive, as a Bounty, FIVE DOLLARS, besides Arms, Cloathing and Accoutrements, and every other Requisite proper to accommodate a Gentleman Soldier, by applying to Lieutenant Colonel ALLEN, or at Captain KEARNY'S Rendezvous, at PATRICK TONRY'S, three Doors above Market-street, in Second-street.

Britain tried to recruit troops among Loyalists in the rebellious colonies. A 1777 handbill offers grants of 50 acres of land and the "polite accomplishments of a soldier" to all recruits. At the war's end, "every gallant hero may retire, and enjoy his bottle and lass."

the Continental Congress," complied at once.

As soon as he could gather some sober men (ninety gallons of rum had been liberated), Arnold took the fort at St. John's. He seized the six-gun sloop *George*, catching seven sailors still in their hammocks.

In this way, without benefit of declaration of any kind, the American Revolution came to Canada. Within another month, the wealthy Virginia squire George Washington had been appointed commander-in-chief of the insurgents. On June 27, he issued formal orders for the invasion of Canada.

nothing but promises

General Guy Carleton had recently told London he needed 10,000 men to protect the colony; what he had that summer of 1775, was fewer than one thousand regulars.

A force of Loyalist settlers, raised from New York and elsewhere by Colonel Allen Maclean, reinforced Carleton's mini-army at a crucial moment, but the governor's effort to raise militia units among the *habitants* met with scant success.

Britain's army had been allowed to run down after the Seven Years' War and now her quartet of generals (Gage, Clinton, Burgoyne and Howe) penned up in Boston, were calling for all possible help. There was nothing for Carleton and Canada, except promises.

The Americans did their best to woo Nova Scotia and Quebec into the republican camp. Both provinces had been invited to the Continental Congress at Philadelphia the previous autumn. When the northern delegates failed to show, the congress sent out a special appeal and a warning:

You are a small people compared to those who with open arms invite you into fellowship. A moment's reflection should convince you which will be the most for your interest and happiness – to have all the rest of North America your unalterable friends or your inveterate enemies.

Washington's personal appeal to Canada was patronizing: "Come then, my brethen, unite with us in an indissoluble union, let us run together to the same goal . . ."

The one-eared Thomas Walker and other Montreal firebrands visited Quebec City to stir up the Protestant community. They fomented trouble in the countryside, trying to set the *habitant* against his *seigneur,* and sowed rumours that the British would deport *Canadiens* in a repeat of the Acadian expulsion two decades earlier. On the other hand, the Bishop of Quebec ordered that any Catholic who joined with the invaders be denied rites of the church – including marriage and the last sacrament. Caught between fires, confused by the issues in a struggle that was not their own, the *habitants* generally stayed aloof from the whole affair. They were, however, willing to sell their produce and labour to either side, but for hard coin only.

the invasion begins

It was September, 1775, before Major-General Richard Montgomery, a former British officer, began the invasion of Canada in earnest. At St. John's, Carleton ordered his garrisons on the Richelieu to hold out until the winter could take the forests into its icy fist.

As the siege of the fort at St. John's wore on, Ethan Allen boiled with impatience and raced off with some Green Mountain Boys to seize Montreal, collecting a small band of bribed *habitants* on the way. When met by a single volley from a line of Redcoats, the raiders fled and Allen was frogmarched into captivity, cursing loudly. He was sent to England in irons.

Although cut off from Montreal and Quebec, the British garrison held out for nine weeks but

Many American riflemen looked as bedraggled as the one in this English caricature. A private in the Continental Army had to buy his clothing out of his $7-a-month pay. Most of the men fought in their hunting or farming clothes – only a few regiments had real uniforms.

Montgomery eventually knocked down the flimsy St. John's stockade with guns rafted from Ticonderoga, including a huge mortar "The Old Sow."

Carleton was in Montreal when he heard the news from the Richelieu and that Benedict Arnold had suddenly appeared at the ramparts of Quebec City with six hundred men. Since mid-September, Arnold had been slogging up the Kennebec River from Maine. This route, through bogs, rapids and forest, was once shunned even by Indian war parties. The ordeal had reduced Arnold's strength by nearly half. His tattered, exhausted brigade arrived with nothing bigger than muskets and ran into Colonel Maclean's Royal Highland Emigrants. When Arnold tried to bluff a surrender, Maclean shut the gates of Quebec and told him to go to hell.

daring and silent escape

Montreal was virtually indefensible and Carleton gathered up about one hundred and thirty soldiers and Loyalists and set out in eleven boats for Quebec. The Americans had already hauled cannons to key points where they could cover narrow channels, particularly among the islets of Lake St.-Pierre The guile and rivercraft of Jean Baptiste Bouchette, known locally as "the wild pigeon," slipped a disguised Carleton past the guns on the dark night of November 16. The *Canadiens* paddled with their hands to avoid alerting sentries.

Montgomery's Americans took over Montreal and moved on through Trois Rivières to Ste. Foy. The pro-republican *congressistes* now showed themselves boldly. In early December, as the snows curtained Quebec, Montgomery joined forces with Arnold. For the second time in sixteen years, on the familiar stage of the Plains of Abraham, the fate of Canada was in the balance.

Inside the walls that still showed scars from Wolfe's assault, Carleton's officers mustered about

Yankee Doodle, Dandy

The YANKEY'S Return from CAMP.

FATHER and I went down to camp,
  Along with Captain Gooding,
There we fee the men and boys,
  As thick as hafty-pudding.
    Yankey doodle keep it up,
Chorus.   Yankey doodle, dandy,
    Mind the mufic and the ftep,
    And with the girls be handy.
And there we fee a thoufand men,
  As rich as 'Squire David;
And what they wafted every day,
  I wifh it could be faved.
    Yankey doodle, &c.
The 'laffes they eat every day,
  Would keep an houfe a winter:
They have as much that I'll be bound
  They eat it when they're a mind to.
    Yankey doodle, &c.
And there we fee a fwamping gun,
  Large as a log of maple,
Upon a ducid little cart,
  A load for father's cattle.
    Yankey doodle, &c.
And every time they fhoot it off,
  It takes a horn of powder—
It makes a noife like father's gun,
  Only a nation louder.
    Yankey doodle, &c.
I went as nigh to one myfelf,
  As 'Siah's underpining;
And father went as nigh again,
  I tho't the deuce was in him.
    Yankey doodle, &c.
Coufin Simon grew fo bold,
  I tho't he would have cock'd it:
It fcar'd me fo, I fhrink'd it off,
  And hung by father's pocket.
    Yankey doodle, &c.
And Captain Davis had a gun,
  He kind of clap'd his hand on't,

And ftuck a crooked ftabbing iron
  Upon the little end on't.
    Yankey doodle, &c.
And there I fee a pumpkin fhell
  As big as mother's bafon,
And ev'ry time they touch'd it off,
  They fcamper'd like the nation.
    Yankey doodle, &c.
I fee a little barrel too,
  The heads were made of leather,
They knock'd upon't with little clubs,
  And call'd the folks together.
    Yankey doodle, &c.
And there was Captain Wafhington,
  And gentlefolks about him,
They fay he's grown fo tarnal proud,
  He will not ride without 'em.
    Yankey doodle, &c.
He got him on his meeting clothes,
  Upon a flapping ftallion,
He fet the world along in rows,
  In hundreds and in millions.
    Yankey doodle, &c.
The flaming ribbons in their hats,
  They look'd fo taring fine, ah,
I wanted pockily to get,
  To give to my Jemimah,
    Yankey doodle, &c.
I fee another fnarl of men
  A digging graves, they told me,
So tarnal long, fo tarnal deep,
  They 'tended they fhould hold me.
    Yankey doodle, &c.
It fcar'd me fo, I hook'd it off,
  Nor ftop'd, as I remember,
Nor turn'd about 'till I got home,
  Lock'd up in mother's chamber.
    Yankey doodle, &c.

Ironically, the most famous song from America's war of independence was originally sung in mockery of the Colonies' rag-tag army. These lengthy lyrics, probably penned by a British army surgeon, Dr. Shuckberg, in Boston in 1775, ridicule the troops who have trouble minding "the music and the step." The last stanza has a cowardly patriot retreat to mother's chamber.

**Benedict Arnold
"Turncoat"**

One of the most famous traitors of history was a Connecticut Yankee officer in the Continental Army. Even before war was declared, he led a force of Vermont volunteers against Fort Ticonderoga, and after its capture marched north, hoping to take Quebec. The seige failed and the army was forced to retreat. As an officer, Benedict Arnold was notorious for wining, dining and womanizing, habits that prompted charges of misconduct. Irked by the hearings but still in command, in 1780 he offered to sell West Point to the British. When his treason was found out, he fled to the British and was rewarded with rank and money. After the war he settled in Saint John, N.B., but the Loyalist townsfolk there boycotted his business, and in 1791 burned him in effigy. Given 13,400 acres in Upper Canada, he left the land to his sons, went to live in England and died a pauper in 1808.

The horrors of war in America, and pestilence and famine for their families at home were the lot of British soldiers — and all for sixpence a day. This 1775 engraving shows unusual compassion in a day when soldiers' lives were cheap.

eighteen hundred combatants. They had four hundred sailors and marines from merchantmen and two ships of war, now held fast in the river ice.

Only about five per cent of his force consisted of career soldiers, and Carleton had doubts about holding out until the spring breakup permitted fresh troops to arrive by sea. He wrote in his journal: "We have so many Enemies within a foolish People, Dupes to those Traitors, with the natural Fears of Men unused to war, I think our Fate extremely doutbful."

Before dawn on the last day of 1775, the Americans launched their attack. It turned out to be little more than a turkey shoot. Montgomery led five hundred New Yorkers past Wolfe's Cove in the whirling snow at 4:00 A.M. With a single roar, four cannon blew a murderous blast of grapeshot into the American ranks. Thirteen men died instantly, and their general dropped on top of the heap.

Aaron Burr, later vice-president of the U.S., led the retreat. Attacking on the St. Charles River side, Arnold was shot in the left knee and Captain Daniel Morgan took command. This brigade of six hundred men was soon trapped.

American deserters had betrayed the time of the attack, and Carleton enjoyed his sleep until the assault was under way. He took an early breakfast, then cooly switched his small veteran platoons to the hot spots as runners brought him reports on the action. By 10:00 A.M. it was all over. About two hundred and twenty of the attackers were dead — the deep snow made an exact count impossible — and over four hundred were taken prisoner. The British death toll was six.

For the next four months, while winter ruled the field, the garrison and the people of Quebec stayed comparatively snug, with adequate reserves of food and ammunition, while the Americans out

Years before anaesthesia, casualties of battle faced excruciating pain at the hands of army medics. A tourniquet (right) stopped the bleeding while the wounded limb was sawn off and the stump was cauterized with a red-hot iron.

on the plains – although reofficered and reinforced – shivered, sickened and suffered.

Inside the fortress, the dragging weeks were lightened by dinners, parties and dances. Relations between the French and British educated classes had flourished. A British officer wrote home:

Their young ladies take the utmost pains to teach our officers French; with what views I know not, if it is not that they may hear themselves praised, flattered and courted without loss of time.

When Scottish regulars had turned out in sub-zero weather in their regimental kilts, the nuns at the Hôtel-Dieu knitted long stockings for them.

The dances of the *seigneurs* and their ladies were the stately minuet and the more spirited quadrille, and the British officers were adept at these formal manoeuvres. Those who had been stationed in the Thirteen Colonies introduced the Virginia Reel, an adaptation of the old English country dance known as the "Sir Roger de Coverley." The *habitants*' furious stepdance to a rasping fiddle and the British sailors' hornpipe shook the taverns of the Lower Town.

Off-duty men crowded the licensed inns and wineshops, and local entrepreneurs opened illegal bars serving moonshine in kitchens or behind small shops – the first speakeasies. Any soldiers suspected of drinking in these dives were given the option of disclosing the address, or twenty lashes. The upper-crust did their drinking at private homes, in the military mess, or at the Freemason's Hall at the top of the curiously named Mountain Hill. Both Richard Montgomery and Benedict Arnold, now in the snows outside the city walls, had roistered at the Freemasons' in earlier days.

Out in the American bivouacs and billets, as in

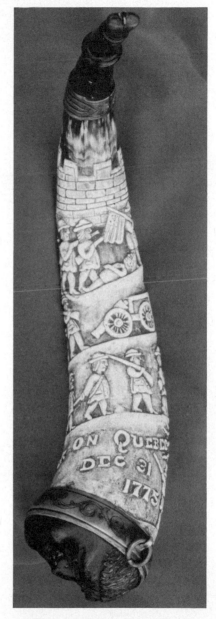

Legend has it that this ornately-carved powder horn was made by a soldier in Montgomery's army who later became a Trappist monk. It shows the American attack on Quebec City in 1775, and bears the words "monk of La Trappe" on the base.

The American invaders brought their Continental dollars to Quebec, but had trouble buying anything with them – only hard coin satisfied the shrewd habitants. *The expression "not worth a continental damn" soon gained currency in Montreal markets.*

the stone buildings of the British fortress, almost everyone played card games. The popular games were piquet and various forms of whist, the forerunner of bridge. Piquet, an intricate two-handed game using thirty-two cards (seven to ace in each suit) was a favorite medium for head-to-head gambling.

A weekly account of life in the beleaguered colony ran in the four-page Quebec *Gazette.* The paper carried all official announcements, some advertisements, and whatever news the regime deemed suitable. No one complained that it fell short of its promise "to introduce every remarkable event, uncommon debates, extraordinary performances, and interesting turn of affairs . . . " Despite the state of war, news trickled in from Newfoundland, Halifax and from the forts at Niagara and Detroit.

Although the American force in Canada grew to over four thousand men, a second effort to storm Quebec was never made. Smallpox ravaged the besiegers, the frost claimed fingers and toes, and officers quarreled. They had no artillery capable of breaking open the walls. Arnold, "the Connecticut horse jockey" (as Carleton called him), had retired to the comforts of Montreal where none other than Ben Franklin, now seventy, was trying to swing the mass of *Canadiens* to the republican cause.

hard cash only

If the *habitants,* torn in their own conflicts of loyalty, had wavered here and there, they were now everywhere disillusioned with their American liberators. A calèche driver in Montreal refused to take a fare from Franklin in the paper dollars of the Continental Congress. Out in the countryside, farmers rejected American money as payment for foodstuffs.

Support drummed up by the *congressistes*

melted away after Montgomery's defeat, particularly as the touch of warmth in the air brought the opening of the St. Lawrence closer every day.

On the morning of May 7, 1776, everyone in Quebec leapt out of bed when news of a ship beating past the Île d'Orleans flashed through the streets. People ran cheering, half-dressed, to the docks. It was the British frigate *Surprise,* and she was shortly followed by *Isis* and *Martin.* It was the vanguard of a fleet bringing fresh troops, weapons and stores.

with pipes and drums

Carleton marched out of the gates of Quebec, drums beating, pipes skirling, his Redcoats ready for battle. But the Americans, now led by General John Thomas, the hero of Boston, had no stomach for fight. They fled in a pack: abandoning their sick, leaving meals half-cooked, throwing off any heavy equipment. They didn't really stop until they were within the walls of Ticonderoga, at the head of Lake Champlain. Thomas himself died of smallpox at Sorel. So ended the first American attempt to take Canada.

If the military dominated this sequence of the Canadian saga, it was no less influential in setting the warp and woof of the national fabric. It would have been simple, for one thing, for Carleton's officers to slaughter the retreating Americans. The *habitants,* capable of shooting out a squirrel's eye at a hundred feet, were not slow to swing to the winning side, and the Indians, with arrow, hatchet and musket, could have been beckoned into the fray. But the bitterness arising from such a policy would have lingered for centuries.

Carleton had his eye on a different, higher goal: beyond all quarrels, all bloodshed, the final co-existence of all the peoples of the Americas. He sent his prisoners home with adequate rations, good shoes, stockings and coats, and told them kindly not to try his patience again. For this lack of ruthlessness he was soon to be relieved of his appointment.

With the threat to Quebec removed, the rest of British North American sprang back to life. An American strongpoint at The Cedars, about thirty miles above Montreal, was swept away by a mixed force of forty Redcoats, a hundred Canadians and bands of Mohawk and Caughnawaga Indians. The distant stockades at Niagara, Detroit, Mackinac – even the few isolated posts deep in the Illinois country – broke out their British flags and breathed deeply of the late spring air.

Two days before the American Declaration of Independence was signed, General Sir William Howe landed on Staten Island and chased Washington out of New York. In the Quebec Basin, ship after ship disembarked a splendid new army of eight regiments of infantry and four batteries of artillery. Four thousand German mercenaries (the "Hessians"), supplied by George III's German princely relatives, were known to be on the way. The British lion still had very sharp claws.

winter draws the line

In naval action on Lake Champlain, the American ships were swept aside and only Ticonderoga barred the way into the Hudson Valley. The fort and its precincts were held by the steady, stooping Yankee general, Horatio Gates, another former British officer, with no fewer than nine thousand men. With the leaves of autumn falling along the shore, Carleton decided to let Ticonderoga stand until the next campaigning season. By this act, unknowingly, he drew the future border.

The winter of 1776-77 was notable for a peak of gaiety in the Canadian cities. Hundreds of well-paid, high-spirited young officers competed for the company of any single girls. Sleighrides and skating parties ended in suppers and dances that lasted

The Guns of '76

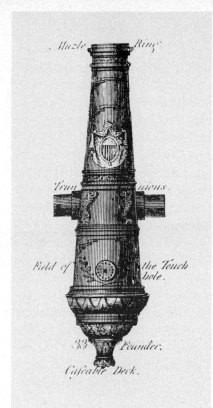

Artillery at the time of America's war of independence was exclusively smooth-bore and muzzle-loading. Ships and forts were equipped with large cannon, up to thirty-three pounders, while smaller, more portable guns were deployed for overland campaigns. Most artillery was loaded with paper or cloth cartridges filled with gunpowder, followed by any of the projectiles shown below: encased grapeshot, bombs, "pine apples," chain shot, or "angels." Ladles were used to load loose charges, ramers to pack the lethal missiles, and spungers to swab the bore after firing. Cannon were fired by igniting a goose-quill tube or quickmatch inserted in the muzzle vent. The backbreaking job of hauling large guns into position was sometimes done by civilians and horses hired only for that purpose, and who fled after the first salvo, leaving the artillery as the booty of the victors. The damage inflicted by these guns varied, of course, with their size and the material with which they were packed. One low-level shot is recorded to have toppled a line of 42 infantrymen, but more often than not, the effects were random and matters of luck rather than accuracy. The American side especially was plagued by shortages of ammunition, and the real victories were won hand-to-hand.

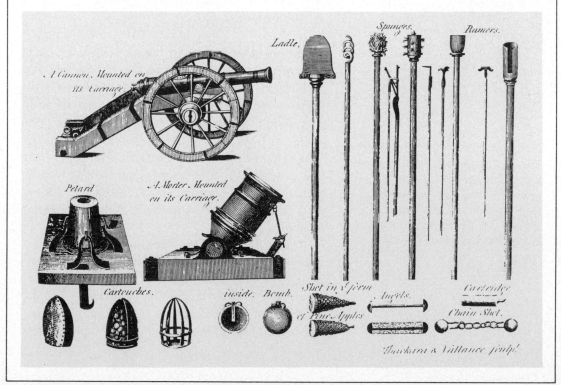

until dawn.

Carleton's caution in pursuit infuriated his second-in-command, Major-General John Burgoyne, a dashing cavalry officer, known universally as "Gentleman Johnny." A poet, playwright and playboy – and a reckless gambler – Burgoyne was a favourite of ruling circles, where Lord George Germain, the minister for the colonies, held an old grudge against Carleton. In London, these two, Burgoyne and Germain, experienced in Eurpoean campaigns but lacking any real knowledge of America, had a wonderful time playing sandbox soldiers. They devised a grandiose scheme to squash the fledgling republic with a few crisp blows. The simple-minded King capered and clapped his hands and Burgoyne was sent back to Canada in the first ship to bring it all to reality. When Carleton learned he was to play no active part in the campaign, he resigned – but had to remain in Quebec for a full year until his replacement arrived.

the best laid plans

Burgoyne was to lead his regiments up Lake Champlain, take Ticonderoga, then, brushing the rabble aside, continue due south down the Hudson Valley to Albany. From New York, General William Howe would strike up the Hudson to join hands, thus splitting off all of New England. From Lake Ontario, for insurance, Colonel Barry St. Leger, a veteran of the Seven Years' War, would obliterate Fort Stanwix in the Mohawk valley, then also proceed to Albany. It all looked great – on paper.

It was July 1, 1777, when Gentleman Johnny appeared at the gates of Ticonderoga. The army he led up Lake Champlain by boat and on foot, heralded by brass bands, fifes and rolling drums, consisted of British regulars in long scarlet coats, waistcoats, tight white breeches and high gaiters;

of German dragoons in cocked hats and jackboots with wide tops; of Canadians in buckskin and homespun; of feathered Indians daubed with warpaint. Each of the regulars carried sixty pounds in weapons and personal gear.

marching in style

The rigours of war? Burgoyne needed thirty carts for his personal supplies, which included his silver tableware, two barrels of wine and two of rum, his mistress and her maid. General Baron von Reidesel, commander of the Hessians, brought along his wife, his children and his servants. Lady Henrietta Acland, like many other officers' wives, accompanied her husband. No fewer than two thousand women travelled with the seven thousand troops. And not only women: bear cubs tamed during the winter lay-over, raccoons, hunting dogs – even a pet eagle.

The fort at Ticonderoga was surrendered by General Arthur St. Clair, another of Washington's ex-British officers, after a brief bombardment from an overlooking crag. To the echo of the guns Burgoyne was cheered by his men for recapturing the fort where the American attack on Canada had begun two years earlier. In London, George III ran into the bedroom of Queen Charlotte shouting, "I have beaten all the Americans!"

But from that day the great scheme came unstuck. Gentleman Johnny pushed on into the swampy watershed of the Hudson, instead of taking the known route along the ribbon of Lake George and thence by road. His overburdened soldiers, maddened by black flies and mosquitos, bravely floundered in mud and bush, hauling their guns and baggage, building corduroy bridges as they went. One bridge was two miles long.

The British march discipline, and the lack of pickings, soon discouraged the Indians and most of the Canadians; the forlorn Germans could not

Two key positions for infantrymen are illustrated in a British drill manual: charge and fire. Some authorities felt that five years drilling was needed to turn a recruit into a disciplined soldier.

communicate with friend or foe; and the support and supplies that Burgoyne and Germain expected from Loyalist farmers did not materialize. Food was seriously short. Colonel St. Leger had failed to take Fort Stanwix and had been chased away by the ubiquitous Benedict Arnold. Much worse, incredible even, the minister for the colonies had simply forgotten to send off orders to Howe in New York to proceed up the Hudson.

On September 13, Burgoyne gamely but foolishly crossed the Hudson, to run headlong into General Gates' army, now twelve thousand men, holding Bemis Heights. A month later, to avoid a slaughter, he surrendered his entire force, reduced to thirty-five hundred effective troops.

For many, this was the turning point of the American Revolution. Washington had lost both New York and Philadelphia, and the testing winter at Valley Forge was soon to come. But American generals and their civilian soldiers had for the first time beaten the British in a set-piece battle. Flagging republican spirits were recharged.

The French saw a chance to strike at hated England; they signed an alliance with the new republic. Spain followed this lead, then Holland. Washington made certain the French had no chance to regain a foothold in Canada, although the appeals of his ally, the dashing young Lafayette, rekindled hopes among those *Canadiens* and *congressistes* who, for their various reasons, wanted to be rid of the British. Forced labour demanded of the *habitants* had soured relations. Carleton wrote prophetically, "There is nothing to fear from the Canadians so long as things are in a state of prosperity; nothing to hope from them when in distress."

The War of Independence dragged on for another four years. Loyalist rangers kept the frontier aflame until the final days but no more armies marched to or from the northern fringe.

The Blockhouse

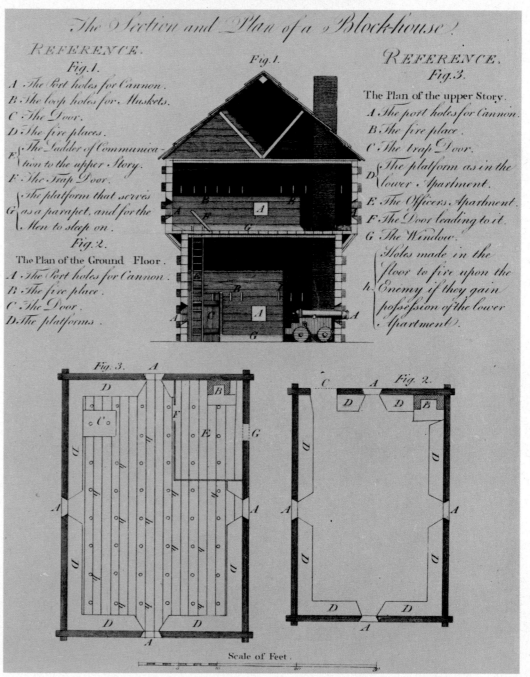

Since most major battles in the Revolution were fought in the open, fixed defences played a minor role in the outcomes. This plan for a blockhouse shows musket loopholes and cannon ports on both floors. The top floor overhangs the first so that defenders could shower their fire on the heads of attackers. Most forts in the colonies were relics of French-Indian wars.

The Fate of Generals

"Gentleman Johnny" Burgoyne's ill-fated attempt to divide and conquer the American colonies ended with his surrender at Saratoga to Horatio Gates, a man he once called "the Old Midwife."

It is the fate of generals that their heroics and blunders decide the outcome of wars. In the American Revolution, the British were led by career officers; the Americans by a hastily gathered lot (mostly British trained) including a bookseller (Henry Knox), a druggist (Benedict Arnold, who later went over to the British), a surveyor (George Rogers Clark), a forge manager (Nathanael Greene) and a frontier fighter (George Washington). Yet it was the British generals who made the telling blunders and the U.S. commanders that provided the bulk of the heroics. On the British side, Thomas Gage dallied and allowed Washington time to form the U.S. army; William Howe lost 1,054 men, killed or wounded, to gain the useless Breed's Hill, and twice took long sea voyages when direct land attacks might have changed the tide; Charles Cornwallis repeatedly let Washington escape before having to surrender to him at Yorktown. "Gentleman Johnny" Burgoyne led his army, entourage and mistress needlessly through dense wilderness before being forced to surrender at Saratoga. Only Guy Carleton's cool head saved Canada from slipping into the republic. For the rebel states, Clark marched his small force 180 miles across frozen swamps in 18 days to take Ft. Stanwix; Greene's brilliant guerilla warefare saved the South; and Washington time and again rallied the faltering rebel cause.

American artist John Trumbull's Death of General Montgomery at Quebec *is typical of "deaths-of-generals" paintings. On New Year's Eve, 1775, Montgomery was shot through the left cheek and legs while leading his troops through a blinding snowstorm toward the city. Red coats seen here are the spoils of war.*

Nova Scotia received a flood of about 30,000 United Empire Loyalists – almost double the size of her existing population – in the great migration of 1783. Some settled around Annapolis Royal, left vacant after the expulsion of the Acadiens several decades earlier. The U.S. never compensated the "disloyal" UELS.

CHAPTER THREE

The Neutral Yankees

We have upwards of one hundred licensed houses and perhaps as many more which retail spiritous liquors without license; so that the business of one half the town is to sell rum and the other half to drink it.

Anonymous resident of Halifax, 1760

The frigate *Albemarle* was beating down the coast of Nova Scotia under full canvas. It was high summer, 1782, the kind of weather–lofty white clouds over long blue rollers– that can make the Maritimes seem like paradise on earth. But as the twenty-eight gun man o' war sliced through the crests, the duty crew were sharply alert. They were hunting American pirates.

The captain, an English parson's son named Horatio Nelson, had brought his ship from Quebec to punish those New England skippers who, since the outbreak of the American rebellion, had been raiding the Atlantic, Bay of Fundy and Gulf of St. Lawrence sea lanes. Led by the notorious John Paul Jones, they were supposed to be cutting British supply routes in support of Washington's armies but in truth they were mostly out for plunder.

Until naval protection arrived, the Americans seized many unarmed ships and mounted looting raids at Annapolis, Liverpool, Lunenburg, Yarmouth, Pictou, Canso, Charlottetown and other ports. They ransacked shops and warehouses, and ripped up the floorboards of homes to steal hidden silver or anything else of value. In a raid at Lunenburg in 1782 the pirates were outwitted by a Negro housekeeper who hid her employer's valuables under her vast skirts, sat down in the kitchen and bawled loudly until the thieves gave up.

Leading citizens were held ransom at pistol-point, and some notables were carried off to Boston. For a brief period, while the Royal Navy was busy off Long Island, the freebooters lay in wait right outside Chebucto Heads to grab coastal freighters emerging from Halifax.

Captain Nelson, at twenty-four, had already shown something of the genius that would win Trafalgar, and something of the passion that would win Lady Hamilton. During a month ashore in Canada he became infatuated with Mary Simpson, the sixteen-year-old daughter of a Quebec garrison officer. When the impetuous sailor seemed determined to marry the girl, so the story goes, he was unceremoniously bundled back aboard the *Albemarle* and taken to sea; his colleagues were horrified that he might ruin his career by marriage to a penniless nobody.

Nelson swept the seas from Cape North to Cape Cod until his men showed signs of scurvy. By then the *Albemarle* was not alone. The tables were turned when the Nova Scotians, most of them of Massachusetts birth or descent, realized that their Yankee cousins were not going to allow kinship to deter them from easy pickings.

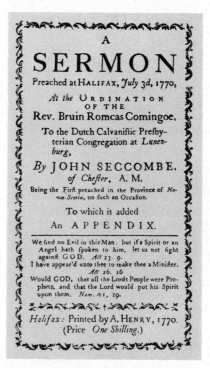

The first religious work published in Nova Scotia was a 1770 sermon preached for the ordination of a Dutch Calvinistic minister with the curious name Bruin Romcas Comingoe, of Lunenburg, the heart of German and Dutch settlements.

Many newcomers to Nova Scotia had enjoyed wealth and position in American cities. However, some had difficulty living up to the motto on the Loyalists' banner once they reached the backwoods of the colony.

The British colonial authorities agreed to commission armed schooners to patrol the inshore waters, one of the first in action being the *Loyal Nova Scotian*, with eight guns. She was joined by the *Buckram*, the *Insulter*, and soon by the *Enterprise*. The last, owned by citizens of Liverpool on the Canadian Mersey, captured seven American vessels on her first voyage; her example was followed by dozens of Bluenose captains, some of whom ranged right down to Florida and the West Indies.

licence to pirate

Most of this "Jolly Roger navy," on both sides, sailed under flimsy authority (known as "letters of marque") sometimes issued by a village council. Crews enlisted in Nova Scotia for these adventures were exempt from the navy press gangs scouring the streets and taverns for single men to "press" into His Majesty's service:

All gentlemen volunteers, seamen and able-bodied landsmen who wish to acquire riches and honour are invited to repair on board the Revenge, private ship of war, now lying in Halifax harbour . . . bound for a cruise to the southward for four months against the French and all His Majesty's enemies.

With Britannia ruling the waves (most of the time), about fifty prize ships a year were taken to Halifax, where both vessels and cargoes were sold at auction at great profit. The captured crews were usually permitted to escape.

When the smouldering discontent in the Thirteen Colonies first burst into flame, all the rebel leaders thought that Nova Scotia would become the fourteenth stripe on the Grand Union flag. It was a reasonable assumption. In 1775 Nova Scotia included all the territory of old French Acadia – including much of the Gaspé, all of present New Brunswick and some part of Maine. The New

Englanders had already conquered the place twice, in 1710 and 1746, and it had been at their insistence that Britain had created the fortress and base at Halifax in 1749.

Two-thirds of the white population of fifteen thousand were Yankee settlers, most of them in the colony for less than twenty years. They were spread thinly along the Atlantic face of the peninsula, close to the cod-fishing grounds, and all around the Bay of Fundy on farms originally broken in by the Acadians. They governed their settlements in the New England way – by town meeting where every man could have his say. In Halifax itself they were engaged in most of the commerce; the ruling group of British officers and bureaucrats shared the upper-class contempt for those "in trade."

Some other distinct groups in the province had little reason to oppose any concerted American take-over bid. The Germans and Huguenots of Lunenburg County spoke little English and, like the surviving groups of Acadians, were not caught up in the complex currents of Britain's European war. The considerable number of Irish were of dubious loyalty. The Indians, Micmac and Malecite, about three thousand of them, once fervent supporters of the French, were now ready to ally with any faction that offered gifts.

ruling the waves

But the dominant factor in Nova Scotian fortunes was always British naval supremacy. After the French fortress, Louisbourg, on Cape Breton had been taken in 1758, Halifax was the power pivot of Britain in America. Nova Scotians had all seen or heard of the great tall ships crowding into Chebucto, the snouts of countless cannon black and menacing, the Redcoat regiments marching ashore with steel bayonets. They had watched Wolfe's battalions go singing aboard the trans-

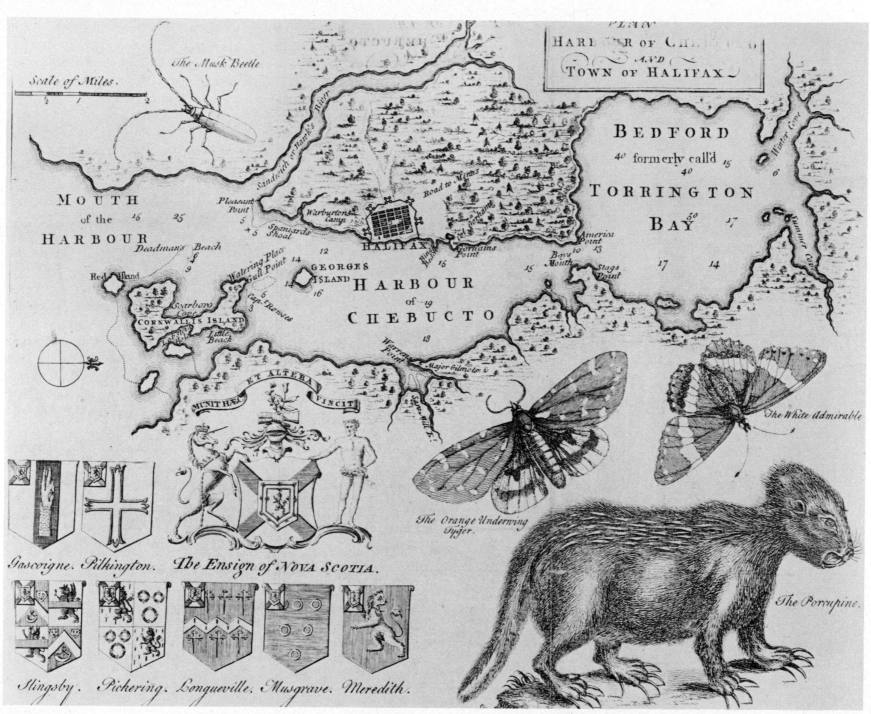

The Musk Beetle

Scale of Miles.

MOUTH
of the
HARBOUR

BEDFORD
40 formerly call'd
TORRINGTON
BAY

Sandwich or Hawk's River

Road to Minas

Pleasant Point

Warburtons Camp

Col. Gorhams

HALIFAX

Deadman's Beach

Spaniards Shoal

America Point

Watering Place

GEORGES ISLAND

HARBOUR
of
CHEBUCTO

Red Island

Scarboro Cove

CORNWALLIS ISLAND

Little Beach

Warrens Point

Bays Mouth

Stags Point

Gull Point

Cap. Rouses

Major Gilmots

MUNIT HÆC ET ALTERA VINCIT

The Orange Underwing Tyger.

The White Admirable

Gascoigne. Pilkington.   The Ensign of NOVA SCOTIA.

Slingsby.   Pickering. Longueville. Musgrave. Meredith.

The Porcupine.

Butterflies, crests, a beetle and a peculiar porcupine cover the wilderness areas surrounding tiny Halifax. Chebucto is the Micmac word for "great long harbour."

39

Nova Scotia's 1767 township census recorded 104 Negroes, 28 Indians and 13,242 Whites.

ports in the spring of 1759 bound for Quebec, and they knew there was nothing either in Boston, New York or Charleston to deny the British force.

To the relief of the governing clique in their fine stone houses on Halifax's Citadel Hill, the majority of the population turned a deaf ear to the republican appeals, thus becoming the neutral Yankees of Nova Scotia.

Forts and blockhouses were strengthened and every cannon primed. The American flag would not get its fourteenth stripe from here; instead, the descendants of "His Majesty's Yankees" were to become almost more British than the British.

first of many to come

In March of 1776, Halifax was suddenly swarming with Redcoats again. General William Howe made the snap decision to abandon Boston where his army had been besieged all winter. He knew that his brother, Admiral Richard Howe, would soon be arriving from New York with a new army and that reinforcements were on the way to Quebec. A do-or-die stand in Boston made no sense.

When the British retired to Halifax, the convoys carried five thousand men, a mountain of military stores (ten thousand barrels of strong ale had recently arrived from England) and every type of household equipment. Officers of that day travelled in some style and comfort, but much of the cargo belonged to a thousand New England colonists whose loyalty to the Crown would have put them in dire danger as Washington's men took the now undefended Boston. These people, like the few who had rallied to the defence of Quebec, were the first of the new breed soon to be known as Loyalists—with a capital "L."

The population of Halifax doubled overnight. Rents and food prices skyrocketed. The original surveyor, Charles Morris, had laid out only a dozen streets with sixteen house lots to the block, but the town had spread up the slopes towards the great hilltop fortress. Frame shanties and cottages reached towards the North West Arm and to The Narrows leading into Bedford Basin. The fashionable Mall had been planked all the way from the Grand Parade to the Kissing Bridge. Argyle Street with its shady willows was the "best" street.

The refugees, many of them well-to-do, filled the Pontac, Golden Ball, Blue Bell and other hotels and taverns, the churches of St. Paul's and St. Matthew's, pitched elaborate tents on the Common or lived aboard ships in the harbour. The main streets – Hollis, Barrington, Sackville, Granville – swarmed with soldiers and sailors from the barracks and encampments, and the bars and brothels on Water and Barrack Streets were roaring day and night. The Spread Eagle (also known as the "Split Crow") on Salter Street was a buccaneer hang-out.

humans bought and sold

The leading citizen of Halifax was Michael Francklin, a merchant and landowner who had married into the wealthy Faneuil family of Boston. The Francklins had brought artists up from New York to decorate the reception rooms in their mansion on Buckingham Street. Blacks from the West Indies did the chores, with competition from the poor whites from Britain who were brought across under contracts which bound them to their masters for years. Humans were bought and sold without fuss:

To be sold at public auction on Monday at the house of Mr. John Rider, two slaves, a boy and a girl about eleven years old; likewise a puncheon of choice cherry brandy with sundry other articles.

In another *Halifax Gazette* advertisement, Mr. John Rock offered two silver dollars reward for the return of his runaway slave, a Negro girl named Thursday. She had fled with a red petticoat and nightdress, and with a red ribbon in her hair. Mr. Jacob Hurd was more generous: he offered five pounds sterling for the return of his Negro slave, "a thickset strong fellow" named Cromwell.

the wine and rum flowed

The three-story Pontac Hotel, operated by John Willis on Duke Street, was a favourite of all the early heroes of the Maritimes, and it saw some heroics of its own. At one dinner for military gentlemen exactly 120 bottles of wine were consumed by forty-seven diners, and they topped that off with half a bottle of brandy per man. Willis charged five shillings a bottle for Madeira, the same for claret and an extra half-crown for brandy. Dinner began at 4:00 P.M. and ran till midnight or later. Willis would supply musicians at ten shillings each. Ale was provided for the batmen who waited patiently to assist their masters homeward, lantern in hand. At another memorable party, the gentlemen drank twenty-eight bumper toasts – that is, at each toast the whole glass had to be emptied, standing.

Almost everyone drank too much. Rum from the molasses of the Caribbean was so cheap that tradesmen set out a barrel of it, complete with tin cup, so that customers could help themselves. Most households had a barrel in the cellar. Two Halifax distilleries turned out ninety thousand gallons a year. A new settler writing home said of Halifax that the business of half the town was selling rum and of the other half, drinking it.

The prosperous merchants and the bureaucrats fattening on government contracts (which they awarded to themselves) could add exotic liquors and pastries to their diets but, from November to May, both rich and poor alike lived basically on salt fish and meat.

Despite the sparse population of the province in 1760, Halifax already boasted of over 100 grog shops, and when not calling for ale, patrons might down a flagon of grog – water and rum. The term originated with Admiral Vernon of the British navy. His sea-hardened crew, used to the daily tot of neat spirits, applied the nickname "Old Grogam" to Vernon for his habit of wearing a Grogam coat, but more to the point, for his nasty habit of watering down their usual ration of rum to grog.

For GLASGOW,

THE SHIP

RUBY.

Now loading at St. John's, New-Brunswick; will call at Halifax, and may be expected by the 10th of December.—She will stop only a few days, and then proceed for Glasgow.—For Passage apply to

WILLIAM FORSYTH and Co.

Halifax, Nov. 18, 1790.

To be Sold,

A NEW HOUSE (partly finished) and A LOT, being the Corner on the Street leading from the Parade to the Citadel, and the upper Cross Street.

Enquire of EDWARD PRYOR, South end of Water-Street.

Halifax, Nov. 18, 1790.

At Public Auction,

By *the Sheriff of the County of Sydney*,

On WEDNESDAY the 9th Day of FEBRUARY next, at three o'Clock in the Afternoon, at the House of WM. GRANT, in GUYSBOROUGH;

SEVEN HUNDRED ACRES of LAND, lying at a place called Goose Harbour, on the North side of Chedabucto Bay, being part of Lot 59; taken by execution at the suit of George Strahan against James Gredy—the time of redemption by law being expired.

Guysborough, November 8, 1790.

To be Sold or Let,

THE Dwelling-House, Barn, Wharf, Stores and Premises, lately occupied by Captain ABBOTT, situate in Water-Street, in the North Suburbs of Halifax.— —For further Particulars enquire of

ELIZABETH M'DANIEL, or CONSTANT CONNER.

Halifax, November 23d, 1790.

Halifax had three newspapers in 1790, when the Journal *carried these advertisements. Since they reached only 2,000 subscribers in all, word-of-mouth was still in business.*

Complexions and teeth suffered and, in a time of rudimentary sanitation, deaths from dysentery, diphtheria, puerperal fever, tuberculosis, typhus and smallpox were common. Anyone over thirty was middle-aged. Lice were so widespread, they were hardly worth comment. The black "beauty patches" of elegantly gowned ladies were, in reality, there to cover smallpox scars and other skin blemishes. Most people thought bathing the entire body was wicked or dangerous, or both; the rich tried to cloak body odours with "Florida water" and imported perfumes, while the poor just stank.

for the rich, by the rich

There was a different justice for rich and poor, as well. A woman who stole five shilling's worth of pots and pans was branded on the hand (T for thief) and jailed. For minor crimes a jacktar, or private soldier, would be flogged with the cat o'nine tails—250 lashes was not uncommon. The maximum a man could stand was set at 1,000. For a felony a serviceman would be shot, or hanged from a ship's yardarm. A civilian could be hanged for petty burglary, and twelve were strung up in public in a single year, one for stealing potatoes.

On the other side of the social register a Sicilian marquis, a soldier of fortune in the militia, found guilty of the rape of a child, was sentenced to walk up and down the Mall for an hour on a cold day with a placard pinned to his uniform. An officer who ran an old schoolmaster through with his sword was acquitted—the victim had had the nerve to come looking in the officers' quarters for his missing daughter.

In the spring and autumn, the well-to-do raced their thoroughbred horses on the North Common, a sport first organized on Canadian soil by Lord William Campbell. Horses were imported from Ireland and from the American south, and the wagering was wild. Hare-coursing, cock-fighting, and hunting and fishing with Indian guides were other popular sports.

A stud farm was established on the fine grasses around Windsor, on the Avon River, and racing was held there also. In its sheltered position near Minas Basin, forty miles from the capital, Windsor was developing as a fashionable summer resort and educational centre. Around this hub, those favoured by the Crown received grants of up to seven thousand acres of the best land.

The Georges of England were of the House of Guelph, rulers of the Duchy of Brunswick in Hanover, and the Germanic relatives supplied troops for most of the 18th-century struggles in America. Haligonians became accustomed to the blue-coat "Hessians" marching stiffly on the Grand Parade. The soldiers wore pigtails, encased in an eelskin, but their officers matched any of Britain's for style and grandeur. The regal Baron de Seitz rode in his own coach-and-four, acknowledging the salutes of the *hoi polloi* with a wave of his diamond-studded hand. To the English-speaking majority, all the *Deutsche* were "Dutch," and thus the province eventually had its Dutchtown and Dutch Village.

one last try

When General Howe took his regiments off to New York, Nova Scotia was left with only three battalions, some of them local militia poorly equipped and trained. It was enough, however, to brush aside the one effort that was made to add the province by force to the new republic.

General Washington had already rejected a scheme for the invasion of Nova Scotia that called for a thousand men to capture Windsor, Fort Cumberland on the Chignecto Isthmus, and the Annapolis Valley, then march overland to take Halifax from the rear. But a band of hotheads based on the border town of Machias decided to have a go on their own. The ringleaders were John

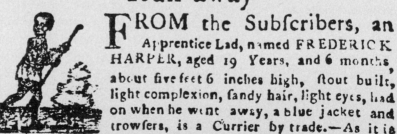
Sales pitches for beer and linen shared an advertising page with a notice about a runaway apprentice. Ship's captains were warned not to "suffer" or aid a likely young stowaway.

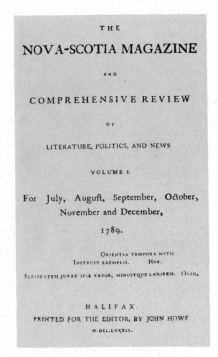

THE

NOVA-SCOTIA MAGAZINE

AND

COMPREHENSIVE REVIEW

OF

LITERATURE, POLITICS, AND NEWS

VOLUME I.

For July, Auguſt, September, October,
November and December,
1789.

ORIENTIA TEMPORA NOTIS
INSTRUIT EXEMPLIS. HOR.

SCRIBENTEM JUVAT IPSE FAVOR, MINUITQUE LABOREM. OVID.

HALIFAX.
PRINTED FOR THE EDITOR, BY JOHN HOWE.
M.DCC.LXXXIX.

The Nova-Scotia Magazine appeared *in 1789 and lasted but three years. Its contents consisted mainly of news and reviews reprinted from British journals, with occasional pieces by the colony's fledgling writers and poets. Its editor and printer, John Howe, was a Loyalist who had learned the trade at the* Boston News Letter, *and had come to Halifax in 1781 to establish the Halifax* Journal. *It was in the* Journal's *print shop that his son Joe gained his apprenticeship.*

Allan, a Scottish settler, Jonathan Eddy, a fugitive member of the Nova Scotian Assembly, Isiah Boudreau, an *Acadien*, Zeb Rowe, Sam Rogers and Obadiah Ayers, all New Englanders.

Colonel Eddy led his liberation army up the Fundy shore in the late fall of 1776. He had gathered a few men along the Maine coast, a few more at Maugerville on the St. John River, more at Shepody and Sackville. Many were armed only with fowling pieces. Some Irish on the isthmus, fooled by rumours about the imminent arrival of a large American army, threw in with the rebels. With this motley force, Eddy decided to attack Fort Cumberland (the old French stronghold, Beauséjour), which barred the land route into the Nova Scotian peninsula. Yorkshire settler Charles Dixon rode non-stop to take the news to Halifax.

Cumberland was manned by about two hundred of the Royal Fencibles, under Colonel Joseph Goreham, himself of New England origin. They simply sat tight through two fumbling assaults until the arrival by sea of reinforcements. In a surprise sally on November 29, the invaders were swept away and their supporters rounded up. Allan halted at the St. John, but Eddy didn't look back till he reached Machias.

The following summer, General Eyre Massey, in command at Halifax, sent three warships to the mouth of the St. John – the site of modern Saint John, N.B. – where his troops swiftly dispersed Allan's last-ditch supporters. Major Gilfred Studholme chased Allan upriver to beyond the site of Fredericton, where the Malecite chief Pierre Tommo switched loyalties and joined the British in the final rout. Eddy got the same treatment when John George Collier took a naval squadron to Machias and reduced the town to ashes. The invasion of Nova Scotia was over.

When the War of Independence itself ended, following the victory on Chesapeake Bay, British North America was pushed back behind lines drawn in Paris. There were highly placed officials in London who would have signed *all* Canada away with a stroke of the pen. At this time, Britain's commerce with Canada was worth less than her trade with the island of Jamaica.

The Atlantic colonies were effectively cut off from central Canada by the northward extension of Maine – a deft trick pulled on the Imperial Commissioners with bland talk of watersheds and heights of land. In a fog of British ignorance, the 45th parallel of latitude was accepted, without real concern, as the border east of the Great Lakes – and this was used, cleverly, to take Lake Champlain, that most Canadian of waterways, wholly into the republic.

Even on the moral issues, the Britishers were easily fobbed off. The peace treaty stated that all private debts between the erstwhile opponents would be acknowledged as valid, and that the American federal government would "earnestly recommend" to the state assemblies that any Loyalists who had not taken up arms retain their property or be compensated for loss or damage. These were just cynical, empty phrases. In reality, any families that could be tagged with the label "Tory" were hunted out, humiliated and some hanged.

These embittered political refugees trudged through the Allegheny mountain passes to start life over again in the western territories, or filtered through the Niagara frontier into empty land north of Lake Ontario. But the great majority were drawn into the security of Manhattan and the other islands at the mouth of the Hudson River which the British held until close to Christmas, 1783. Everybody who wanted to go – both military and civilian – was shipped, bag and baggage, to Nova Scotia.

This view of downtown Halifax in 1777, sketched by Richard Short of the Royal Navy, shows St. Mather's Meeting House (left) and the Governor's House. (centre) on Hollis Street. Looking up George Street, Citadel Hill is faintly visible. The two taverns (left and right) are just opening up for business.

45

Garrison Life

Wherever posted, garrisons became the focal point of local social activity. Actual combat was infrequent for the officer-gentleman, usually among the best-educated and most sophisticated of the populace. When not involved with drilling, guard duty or mock battles, soldiers sought diversion. The Redcoats produced theatricals, played cricket, skated, held regattas, gave dances at the mess, drank vintage wines and competed for the favours of the town's young ladies.

While troops of the garrison at Fort George, Upper Canada, go through their daily drill, two soldiers tend to the garrison's mascots – black bear cubs.

"A spot called the garrison, stands on a bank of the main land . . . and consists only of a wooden block-house, and some small cottages of the same materials, little superior to temporary huts. The house in which the Lieutenant-governor resides is likewise formed of wood, in the figure of a half square, of one story in height, with galleries in the centre."

George Heriot, *Travels Through the Canadas* (1807)

The beginnings of Toronto — the Fort York barracks: an Indian family arrives to trade while others spear fish. Garrison troops are busy with building and KP.

These Loyalists, camped on the banks of the St. Lawrence River at Johnstown in 1784, came north to Canada carting with them whatever possessions they could manage. The artist, James Peachy, was himself a Loyalist, trained as a draughtsman in Boston, and forced to flee when the revolution erupted in New England.

CHAPTER FOUR

The True Blue Tide

Many hundred had fallen victims to the unrelenting cruelties of the Rebel States, on no other account but that of their allegiance to their Sovereign...

The Case and Claim of the American Loyalists, 1783

"It is, I think, the roughest land I ever saw. We are all ordered to land tomorrow and not a shelter to go under." These nervous words went into the diary of Mrs. William Frost as she sat on the deck of a ship in Saint John harbour on the morning of June 29, 1783.

Five weeks later Sarah Frost gave birth to a daughter. With her husband and family, she represented the thoughts, the fears, of the Loyalists who decided to leave (or were driven from) the newly proclaimed United States.

From unpromising, embittered beginnings, these fifty thousand refugees would multiply and prosper in their new land, soon spreading throughout British North America, pushing back its forest frontiers, creating new provinces, changing the cultural heritage, casting the mould for a separate nation in the north.

They were not the effete collection of snobs, tyrants, bootlickers and bureaucrats pictured in the American populist propaganda. By the time the last British troops left St. Augustine, Savannah, Charleston, New York and Penobscot, most of the colonial aristocrats, the plantation owners and imperial officials had already departed for the British Isles or the West Indies.

A sprinkling of those who chose Canada was, indeed, from well-to-do and long-established families—some of them, like Edward Winslow and John Coffin boasted Mayflower ancestors. At a time when it was unusual for the average man to be able to write his name, there were several hundred university graduates among them, most from Harvard. There was a middle class of merchants, professional men, clergymen and clerks, and a broad band of shopkeepers, farmers, artisans, schoolteachers and labourers. But because free land and rations were being offered in Canada, there was also a fringe of speculators, opportunists and petty criminals.

The United Empire Loyalists were certainly not all united nor all of British stock. Hollanders from upper New York and Pennsylvania, Quakers, Germans, even some French, opted for the King's realm. The migration included those men from the continental European regiments (the Hessians) who wanted to stay in the New World. Negroes were shipped north by the hundreds, technically free men but without any roof except their master's.

The Loyalists who came into Canada were, then, pretty much a wide slice from the most industrious and self-sufficient segment of American colonial society. Carleton had concluded much

THE disinterested PATRIOT CANDIDATES, Friends to the KING and CONSTITUTION.

JONATHAN BLISS,
WARD CHIPMAN,
CHRISTOPHER BILLOPP,
WILLIAM PAGAN,
STANTON HAZARD,
JOHN M'GEORGE.

SAINT JOHN.
PRINTED by C. SOWER.

New Brunswick's first election in 1785 exposed bitter rivalries among the Loyalists. Public voting (there were no secret ballots yet) for candidates listed on election cards (above), split the inhabitants into two factions — the Upper Cove, for rule by the aristocracy, and Lower Cove, for democratic rule.

The immigrant ship Clarendon,
*bound for "Charlotte Town in the
Island of St. Johns, North America,"
carried 125 passengers, among them
15 Campbells, 15 Stewarts,
14 McDonalds and 10 Kennedys.
All the immigrants were labourers,
their wives, sisters and children, and
all listed "want of employment" as
their reason for leaving Scotland.*

earlier that Canada needed an aristocracy as much as it needed powdered wigs and crinolines. The rebellion had attracted the radicals; these were the conservatives.

Each civilian family head was to have a hundred acres, plus fifty more for each member of the family; thus, a family with ten or twelve children, by no means uncommon, began with a sizeable property. And those with funds could buy cheaply as much more as they could afford. Officers quitting the service were treated more liberally (a captain could have seven hundred acres), but these were mostly single men, with little taste or aptitude for farming, and many later abandoned or sold their grants.

the spoils of war

The end of campaigning had left the British with vast stores of salted meat (mostly pork), hard biscuits, flour, tents, guns, tools and all the paraphernalia of a large military establishment. This mountain of material was shipped north where it was doled out carefully to sustain the new settlers over the first few years. There was enough at the outset to ensure each family an axe, hammer and nails, saw and spade; each group of five families shared a gun to shoot game, and a whipsaw to cut house planks.

Three hundred of the luckiest moved into the arable Annapolis Valley, but the great majority from New York were dumped into Halifax by skippers under orders to turn their ships around as fast as possible. Once again, the Chebucto inlet was ringed with tents and every building overflowed. For four months, nearly ten thousand were fed at canteens set up in Halifax streets.

On the fourth of May, 1783, a convoy of thirty ships pressed into the sheltered harbour of Port Roseway. At the head of the inlet at the southeastern tip of Nova Scotia, a town site modelled on Philadelphia had been laid out with five main streets. The authorities had guaranteed survival rations, plus four hundred thousand feet of sawn lumber. The Loyalists disembarked on the heavily forested shores, and the Rev. Jonathan Beecher spoke for most of them when he wrote:

As soon as we had set up a kind of tent, we knelt down, my wife and I and my two boys, and kissed the dear ground and thanked God that the flag of England floated there. We resolved that we would work with the rest to become again prosperous and happy.

When Governor John Parr paid a call on August 2, he was cheered in the streets of the new city, which he named Shelburne in honour of the British prime minister. The portly governor (he weighed 250 lbs.), danced all that night at a ball where the Loyalist ladies, scorning the baying of wolves in the backwoods, waltzed around in low-cut gowns, long gloves, with ivory fans and perfume sachets, precious finery from trunks dragged hundreds of miles from their lost homes along the Hudson or Susquehanna.

moment in the sun

More convoys came to Shelburne that autumn and, with ten thousand residents, it became the most populous place in British North America – at that time, Quebec, Montreal and Halifax had permanent populations of about eight thousand each. Shelburne had two newspapers, two churches, several taverns and a coffee-house.

When Prince William Henry, later to be King William IV, visited in 1785, all Shelburne turned out in a fine show of loyal ardour, but people were already slipping away to more arable areas. When government rations were cut off after three years, the population plummeted to one thousand, then to three hundred. Entire streets of substantial frame houses were abandoned, doors left swinging

50

in the salt breeze. It was a story repeated at Port Mouton and at several other spots along the Atlantic coastline.

The misfortune of "Nova Scarcity" was a windfall to the virtually empty St. John's Island, as Prince Edward Island was then known. Although the deep red soil of the island offered easy farming, development had been frustrated by the British government's stupidity back in 1764. Excepting only three town sites, the island had been sliced into lots of 20,000 acres each, and these divided by lottery among a group of admirals, generals, politicians, bureaucrats and royal favourites.

feudal lords of PEI

These absentee proprietors were supposed to settle at least one European Protestant on every 200 acres within ten years. With very few exceptions, they ignored their obligations.

One of the land-owners actually occupying his "lot" (number nineteen), was Captain Walter Patterson of County Donegal, installed as governor when the island became a separate colony in 1769. He sent an agent to Shelburne, with news of fertile land. About six hundred responded, settling gladly on the sandy loams around Hillsborough and Bedeque Bays, discovering as a bonus that the waters of Northumberland Strait offered the finest shellfish in the world.

The devil in the P.E.I. paradise was "the land question." The feudal landowners refused all requests by the settlers for freehold titles and, although they were getting their lots developed for free, they still tried to collect exhorbitant rents. Many embittered Loyalists, refusing to become anyone's peasants, moved yet again – to Cape Breton, or to the Tantramar marsh county of Chignecto, or up the St. Lawrence to Quebec. Their places were filled by eight hundred penniless Scots sent out by the Earl of Selkirk to farm land he had bought for them.

The second major stream of Loyalists from New York was directed into the fortified harbour of the St. John River. Eight thousand civilians, soldiers from disbanded armies, arrived with their families before Christmas, 1783. One of the ships that carried them was aptly named the *Hope*; others were the *Lady's Adventure*, the *Camel* and the *Grand Duchess of Russia*. A shack town that sprang up close to the ten-acre Hazen and White trading post was called Parrtown, after Governor Parr.

Parr, an ageing soldier looking for a serene retirement, was pleased when the St. John Loyalists won London's approval the following year for the creation of a new province, New Brunswick, connecting to ancient Nova Scotia at the Chignecto Isthmus. There was soon hell to pay when Parr's hurried surveys of town and country were found to be full of errors.

Canada's first city

Colonel Thomas Carleton, younger brother to Guy, was appointed first governor of the true-blue province, and that illustrious name went on another town on the western harbour shore. The next year, 1785, Parrtown and Carleton were incorporated by royal charter as the city of Saint John, the first incorporated city in Canada.

The official plan for the province had inked in town sites at Kingston, Queenstown, Gagetown and St. Anne's. The latter, eighty-four miles up the St. John, was renamed Fredericton and designated provincial capital, much to the chagrin of the merchants of Saint John.

The success story of John Coffin, a settler in the St. John River valley, brightens a period of unremitting toil as the Loyalists, most of them already middle-aged, attacked the forests with little more than hand tools. Born in Boston, Coffin had

**Thomas Carleton
The Governor's Brother**

A career officer following in the footsteps of his older brother, Guy, Thomas Carleton volunteered for the British Army in 1753 at 18, and came to Canada under his brother's command. In 1784, when the new province of New Brunswick was created, he was named governor. He soon ran headlong into conflict with reformers in the Assembly, many of whom were late Loyalists inoculated with democratic ideas brought up from the States. The election of 1793 gave reformers the majority and further loosened Carleton's grip on provincial purse strings. In 1803, he returned to England, but in the custom of the day continued to collect the lieutenant-governor's salary from New Brunswick until his death.

Fences

The earliest settlers used brush, deadwood or piles of slash to mark the boundaries of their land. However, when time permitted it, real fences were built from felled timber, bearing evocative names like snake, zigzag, worm and Virginia rail, seen in detail below.

Unique to North America, a derivative of the Indian hunting fence, the Virginia rail called for stakes at each intersection to keep the heavy top rail in place.

Chock-and-log fences ran in straight lines and could be moved quite easily. Long ends were laid on short cross-pieces, or notched chocks, to hold timbers in place.

Snake, worm or zigzag fence timbers had to be set at wide angles for stability and used up vast amounts of timber, but eliminated the digging of postholes.

Post-and-rail fences used up less timber than other wood fences, but forced farmers to dig postholes. When the uprights rotted, the back-breaking chore was repeated.

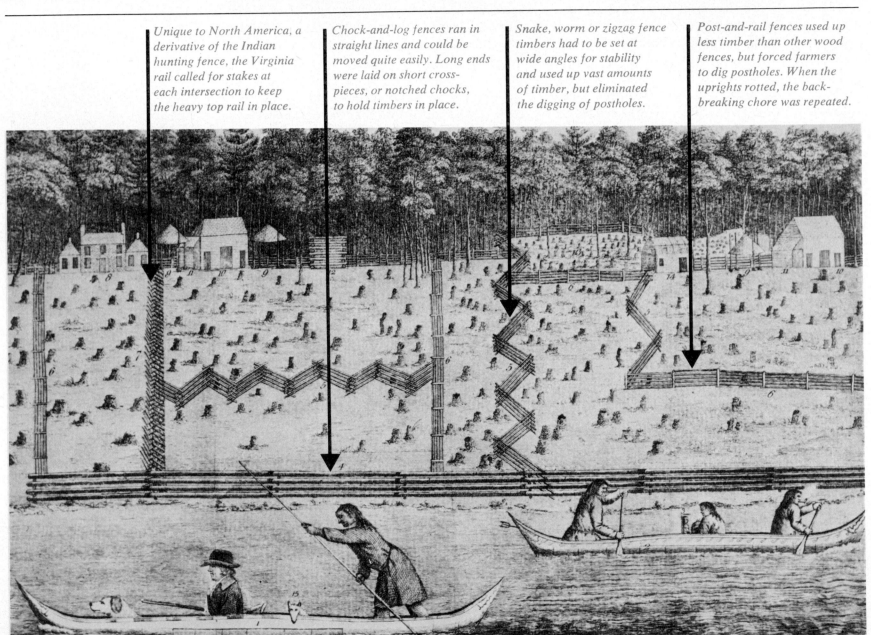

distinguished himself in several battles. After the surrender at Yorktown, he had slipped through the republican lines, a price of $10,000 on his head, to visit his girl, Ann Matthews, near Charleston, then occupied by the enemy.

the enemy skirted

Only minutes after his arrival, a rebel guard pounded on the door. A Redcoat officer had been seen on the grounds. Ann remained seated on a divan. A patrol searched the home, then departed with apologies. When a servant gave the all-clear, Ann stood up, lifted her hoop skirts, and out from under the yards of gingham emerged the grinning Coffin. At six feet, two inches, he had been doubled up in pretty close quarters. John and Ann were married the same year and shortly afterwards boarded a square-rigger bound for Saint John.

Although few of the first generation Loyalist settlers on the St. John ever knew prosperity – getting surplus produce to markets was nearly impossible – Coffin was unstoppable. He built flour mills and saw mills and imported pedigree animals to improve farm stock. When war returned in 1812, he led the New Brunswick Fencibles as a colonel and, at seventy-four was commissioned a general.

The position and condition of the average settler in New Brunswick was well described by a touring British officer:

Any man that will work is sure in a few years to have a comfortable farm; the first eighteen months is the only hard time, and that in most places is avoided, particularly near the rivers, for in every one of them a man will catch enough in a day to feed him for a year. In the winter, with very little trouble, he supplies himself with meat by killing moose-deer; and in summer with pigeons, of which the woods are full. These he must subsist on until he had cleared enough to raise a little grain.

Ever since the British defeat at Saratoga, Loyalists from New England and upper New York had been trekking with ox carts and on foot into Quebec. Others followed the Mohawk Valley to Oswego and Sacket's Harbour on Lake Ontario. There was a steady trickle crossing the Niagara and Detroit rivers, keeping close to the western forts, still held by the British. When the terms of the peace treaty became known, the stream of refugees swelled to a flood.

In July, John Johnson, son of the famous patriarch of the Mohawk Valley, reported that 3,776 persons, 1,492 of them children, had been settled on this land. The total settled by year's end was 6,-152. They were the vanguard of perhaps ten thousand who would take up "The Front," as the north shore of the St. Lawrence River and Lake Ontario soon became known.

"Settled," however, was a bit of a misnomer. Virgin forest came to the water's edge. On the 200-acre lot it was often impossible to find enough open space to build a cabin. There was not a single bridge, nor a mill, nor a mile of road. Families who had left behind fertile, fenced farms and solid, even gracious homes, stood appalled at the task before them. Many possessed only the clothes they wore, and the scanty tools and rations provided from army stores.

gentle, helpful Indians

However harsh the environment, the settlers met only gentleness from the local Mississaugas. The Indians taught the whites how to catch fish with hooked sticks, get sugar from the maple, take nourishment from roots and nuts, and how to prepare hides for clothing or bedding. On many a table, the dishes were Indian birch bowls.

The settler's first shelter was usually a tent or other waterproof cover, with father and the older boys sleeping under the stars around a log fire

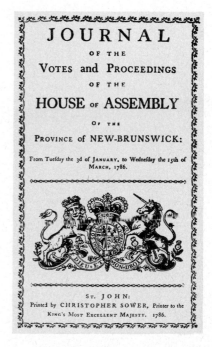

A fine product of the early Canadian press, Christopher Sower's journal of the legislature was published a year after his appointment as King's Printer in the new province.

when the weather permitted. The firelight served to keep black bear and wolves at a distance; the smoke deterred the voracious mosquitoes. As the light ship-axes widened the clearing, timber for a log shanty was piled up. This crude first home was seldom more than ten feet by eight, the roof sloping from about six feet high above the only door, to four feet at the rear wall.

by muscle and friendship

When ready to build, the settler sent his sons along the bush tracks to collect his neighbours. Lacking almost all machinery, even the simplest block-and-tackle, large foundation boulders had to be lowered into place by hand. The notched and peeled basswood or pine logs for the walls were lifted by sheer muscle. No newcomer could exist alone in the forest, and eager co-operation in working "bees" became a marked feature of the Loyalist settlements.

The Loyalist settlers, for the first three years, could fall back on the basic army ration of salt pork, hardtack biscuits and peas, but the industrious among them concocted nourishing meals. A stew of beaver and partridge or pigeon meat, boiled with wild rice and corn, simmered in the black iron cooking pot. A ragoût of venison and potatoes was stretched by adding just about anything edible. Mouths watered as an entire skinned rabbit was lowered into bubbling broth.

The thin margin of security was illustrated graphically during 1788-89 – "the hungry year." The government hand-out ended in 1787, and, as luck would have it, drought, poor crops and an early and severe winter ravaged the settlements.

The distress was acute along the Bay of Quinte. The few cattle and horses, even pet dogs and bull-frogs, were eaten, and seed potatoes already planted were dug up. Children watched the foraging pigs and ate the roots the swine preferred.

All Loyalists who fled to British North America received a grant of land – or did they? This 1785 petition from a freed black man for land and aid shows that not all Loyalists were treated alike.

Buds from maple, beech and basswood were boiled. Near Picton, a single beef bone was passed from house to house for soups. One of the best farms at Hay Bay was offered in exchange for fifty pounds of flour. At least five deaths from starvation were recorded nearby, including a woman found dead with a live baby at her breast. Others died from eating poisonous roots or berries.

When the crisis passed, and more efficient transportation ruled out future famine, the legend was retold around the log fires of how a desperate father left his family in the winter bush to search for food. When he got back eight days later with some supplies, he found wife and children in fine shape. During his absence the family tabby cat, which had never before shown the slightest enterprise, appeared every day with a rabbit.

wilderness transformed

There seemed to be something semi-miraculous, too, in the swift transformation of the forest into a thriving and ambitious community. Among the new names on the map, Adolphustown, at the entrance to the Bay of Quinte, held seniority, settled by the Van Alstines on June 16, 1784. Napanee (1785), Picton (1786), Belleville and Trenton (1790) followed where river or natural harbour offered sites for water-power mills or strategic communications. Schooners now plied Lake Ontario and commerce was beginning to flourish.

As early as 1785, Loyalist leaders began to suggest that Upper Canada should be separated from Quebec so that they could live under British laws and customs, as their fellows were already doing in Nova Scotia and New Brunswick. This movement had gathered strength by the time Lord Dorchester was back at the helm. He had shaped the Quebec Act of 1774 in hopes of winning the confidence of the French-Canadian majority; now it was obvious that the true-blue tide had changed the picture dramatically. After much debate on both sides of the Atlantic, the British Parliament passed the Canada Act in May, 1791.

The old Province of Quebec was cut into halves to form Lower Canada and Upper Canada, along the language and settlement line just above Montreal, and the new provinces were each granted an elected assembly with powers over regional matters.

The man chosen as first lieutenant-governor of Upper Canada, John Graves Simcoe, was a British M.P. who had been colonel of the volunteer New York Queen's Rangers during the revolutionary war. On July 26, 1792, he reached the village of Newark (Niagara-on-the-Lake), where he installed his family in a large tent.

That river was the border with the United States. In Simcoe's eyes it was just a narrow moat separating his Loyalists from the detested enemy. After inspecting the frontier as far as Detroit, he knew the capital must be removed to a more protected site. He first favoured a spot on the Thames River where London would later stand, and put some of his newly-enlisted Queen's Rangers to work cutting an access road (Dundas Street) from Burlington Bay. But, in the spring of 1793, under orders from Lord Dorchester, he inspected the natural harbour at what is now Toronto and agreed to build his capital there.

Except for a clearing where the French had once traded with the Indians, the densely forested shore was deserted, the bay teeming with wildfowl. But the forty-one-year-old Simcoe was a man whose vision was matched by equal energy and self-confidence. He ordered that a future metropolis be marked out amid a grove of large oaks. Before a tree was felled he had demanded a bishop and a university. He called the place York, after the warrior duke of that name.

Monotonous winter meals were forgotten when skies over Fort Erie, U.C., were darkened by huge flocks of wild pigeons in April 1804. Hundreds were easily shot, trapped and netted.

Simon Fraser's canoe tilts down a chute on the turbulent river that now bears his name, on his epic voyage. Fraser mistakenly thought he was on the Columbia.

CHAPTER FIVE

To the Far Oceans

I scarcely ever saw anything so dreary and dangerous in any country, whatever way I turned my eyes, mountains upon mountains whose summits are covered with eternal snow.

Simon Fraser, 1808

Simon Fraser, a stocky red-haired man with the face of "John Bull" and determination to match, had already performed minor miracles in the unexplored canyon of the Rocky Mountain Trench. Racing ever southwards and falling thirteen hundred feet in four hundred miles, the foaming river snatched away his canoes and much of his stores. A paddler in his expedition of twenty-two men was mauled by a grizzly. Suspicious Indians dogged their path. Unnamed tributaries, each a major river, had been recorded plunging into the mainstream. Now, on June 26, 1808, after almost a month of hazard and hardship, the travellers stopped and gaped in awe at the sight before them.

Hell's Gate was an apt name for it. The river (which Fraser mistook for the Columbia) squeezed through a cleft of the Coast Range and exploded forward in a yellow maelstrom. Between high cliffs it was only one hundred and twenty feet wide and nearly as deep. Roaring ceaselessly, it tossed huge logs about like toothpicks. In his journal the normally taciturn Fraser wrote:

I have been for a long period among the Rocky Mountains, but have never seen anything to equal this country, for it is so wild that I cannot find words to describe our situation at times. We had to pass where no human being should venture . . . Where the ascent was perfectly perpendicular, one of the Indians climbed to the summit, and with a long pole drew us up, one after another. This took three hours. Then we continued our course up and down, among hills and rocks, and along the steep declivities of mountains, where hanging rocks and plunging cliffs at the edge of the bank made the passage so small as to render it difficult even for one person to pass sideways.

With his companions John Stuart and Jules Quesnel, the thirty-two-year-old Fraser not only passed through Hell's Gate but continued to follow the great river to the Strait of Georgia. Then, threatened by Cowichan warriors, Fraser turned his back to the Pacific that same evening and began to retrace his journey up the river.

Simon Fraser's journey was only one of the several epic explorations in the first half-century of British rule, but it is typical of many. It was performed by traders looking for new sources of wealth and for navigable rivers leading to world markets, either east or west.

While it was not imperialist in design it opened for exploration areas where boundaries were still vague. In practical terms it was made possible by the guidance and hospitality of the indigenous

When his Loyalist father died in a U.S. prison, Simon Fraser and his mother left their Vermont home for Quebec. In 1801, at age 25, Fraser joined the North West Company as a partner. He established a series of forts to provide a food supply for traders, and selected suitable sites for settlement in what is now British Columbia. In 1801, he left Fort George and began his epic journey by canoe to the Pacific Ocean.

The invention of the sextant in 1731, and three decades of improvements by such men as Isaac Newton, increased the accuracy of maps and ship's logs. Typical of period journals, Archibald Hamilton's notebook of 1763 includes details of voyages to Cape Breton, Quebec and Montreal.

peoples. Although many of the natives these explorers met had never before seen a white face, cooperation was routine and bloodshed rare.

Were these explorers really ordinary men? Young James McDougall went off on snowshoes from the Peace River into the Parsnip and on to Fort McLeod, the first trading post west of the Rockies—plodding three hundred miles through high mountain passes, over frozen rivers and across treetop snowdrifts, carrying his gun and full pack. When his work was done at the post, he pushed farther into the western highlands, discovering the fifty-mile-long Stuart Lake. Among his fellows, such efforts were not considered in any way remarkable.

After the Seven Years' War, the directors of London's competing fur-trading companies turned their eyes to the vast Northwest. A popular map labelled the entire territory beyond Lake Winnipeg, "These parts unknown." But the glossiest furs came down the high western rivers, and there was some evidence that copper and other metals existed in the hinterland. The old dream of a midcontinental waterway to the silks and spices of the Orient still flickered in the minds of both merchants and strategists. The stage was set for the drama of Canadian discovery.

sea-legs at eleven

Samuel Hearne was raised in Dorset, England, and was sent to sea at age eleven, acting as captain's runner in several naval actions. Hardened by icy winds in the rigging and by salt beef in the mess, he was just the kind of young man the Hudson's Bay Company was looking for.

By 1766, Samuel was mate on the company's ships trading out of Fort Churchill, around the rim of the HBC's private inland sea. The blue-eyed sailor caught the eye of Moses Norton, the resident HBC governor—and also the eye of the governor's daughter, Mary.

Norton was trying to find the source of the copper that for fifty years had been seen at the Bay posts in Indian ornaments and knives, and sometimes in nuggets. He knew only that the metal came from some far northern river, close to the frozen seas that had defeated all the attempts by Frobisher, Davis, Hudson, Baffin and others to find the North-West Passage across the top of the continent.

the legendary Matonabbee

Hearne, at twenty-four, was ordered to find those copper mines, while promoting the Bay's business among the Dogrib, Slave, Chipewyan and other tribes known to be scattered across the vast belt of tundra. He was also, of course, to look for any evidence of a passable route to China.

After two abortive journeys that served to sharpen his survival knowledge, we meet Hearne in December, 1770, clad in otter skins. With him is a remarkable Cree chieftain, Matonabbee, who had befriended the Bayman near Dubawnt Lake the previous summer. Matonabbee's cruelty was legendary among white men, but it's very doubtful Hearne could have achieved much of importance without the Indian's protection and assistance.

Matonabbee could converse in the pidgin Cree used by the HBC and he also knew a few English phrases. Enjoying eight wives himself, he explained to Hearne why it was essential they take women along:

Women were made for labour; one of them can carry or haul as much as two men can do. They also pitch our tents, make and mend our clothing, keep us warm at night. There is no such thing as travelling any considerable distance, or for any length of time, in this country without their assistance. Though they do everything, women are maintained at a trifling expense, for as they cook, the very licking of their fingers in scarce times is sufficient for their subsistence.

It was no safari. The size of the party swelled and shrank, depending on the population of the territory traversed and the supply of game. At times it numbered two hundred. Speed was never a factor; often progress was only four miles a day.

They pushed west along the Seal River, swinging out in a wide arc towards Great Slave Lake, keeping just above the tree line. Hearne noted: "On the barren grounds, there is a total want of herbage, except moss on which the deer feed."

days of cold and hunger

Hearne's sensitive and meticulous journal – a remarkable literary achievement from one with only a few years' village schooling – provides a vivid picture of the 18th-century adventurer in his element.

For many days, we had been in great want, and for the last three days had not tasted a morsel of any thing, except a pipe of tobacco and a drink of snow water. Our strength began to fail . . . I could not refrain from wishing myself again in Europe if only to alleviate the extreme hunger with the refuse of the table of any one of my acquaintance.

When caribou were killed, the Indians gorged for a day, each eating enough meat to satisfy six men. Then they would all vomit, solemnly blaming their upset stomachs on bad spirits. Hearne ate just about all the food offered, including raw musk-ox, but drew the line at body lice and warble flies. He also ate the large whooping crane, considered a delicacy by the Indians; it was already rare enough to merit a full description in his notes. The crane's long wingbones, he wrote, were later made into flutes.

**Matonabbee
The Chipewyan Chief**

"The vivacity of a Frenchman . . . the sincerity of an Englishman . . . the gravity and nobleness of a Turk" — that was explorer Samuel Hearne's description of the Chipewyan chief, Matonabbee. And although no known picture exists of him, the portrait of one of his kinsmen (above) could well fit the bill. Born about 1736 at Prince of Wales Fort on Hudson Bay, he grew up as the adopted son of Richard Norton, governor at the fur "factory." His education in European manners, however, did nothing to dull his knowledge of the North. As a trapper he brought in more furs than the others, year after year. He was Hearne's guide on his epic 5,000 mile trek across the Barrens — a man without whom Hearne would never have made it. And he was a diplomat, uniting the Chipewyans, Cree and smaller tribes into the first Dene nation in 1772.

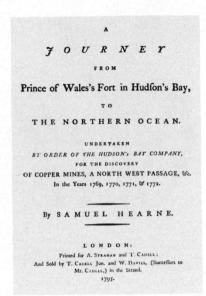

A

JOURNEY

FROM

Prince of Wales's Fort in Hudson's Bay,

TO

THE NORTHERN OCEAN.

UNDERTAKEN

BY ORDER OF THE HUDSON's BAY COMPANY,
FOR THE DISCOVERY
OF COPPER MINES, A NORTH WEST PASSAGE, &c.
In the Years 1769, 1770, 1771, & 1772.

By SAMUEL HEARNE.

LONDON:
Printed for A. STRAHAN and T. CADELL:
And Sold by T. CADELL Jun. and W. DAVIES, (Successors to
Mr. CADELL,) in the Strand.
1795.

*Though Samuel Hearne did not live
to see publication of his account
of his life and journeys (opposite
page), his record is considered one
of the most remarkable documents of
early exploration. While many other
explorers saw the country and the
natives in terms of their official
commission or the problems they had
faced, Hearne's diary and pictures
give not only a precise view of the
land and people of the far north,
but an honest portrait of himself.*

After seven months, Hearne reached the stream he called the Coppermine River, which drains the chain of lakes to the east of Great Bear. He was disappointed to find the river shallow and so full of rocks and rapids that it could barely be used by canoes.

Hearne knew he was five hurdred miles west of Hudson Bay and well above the Arctic Circle, and the Indians said there was no known end to the land still further westward. The sailor from the cobbled hamlets of Dorset marvelled at the hugeness of the continent and stared at the mile-wide strip of open water that washed into the bay: did this open water extend from Atlantic to Pacific, offering a summertime waterway across the top of the world? Half a century later, the entire Franklin expedition would be lost in search of the answer.

just rocks and gravel

Fearing Eskimo reprisals for his own depredations, Matonabbee would not permit Hearne to dally. There was time only to throw up a rock cairn, claiming possession for the HBC (the town of Coppermine, N.W.T., stands at that spot today). And the copper? The Indians took Hearne to the "mine"–just "a jumble of rocks and gravel, rent many ways by an earthquake." It was of no commercial interest, but Hearne picked up a few ore samples to take back with him. The return journey, meandering in the Indian style, going to where the game was, took no less than ten months.

With expected modesty, Hearne slipped back into his role as a Bayman. Two years later, with Matthew Cocking, he established Cumberland House, on Pine Island Lake, just about where the border of Manitoba and Saskatchewan would be drawn some one hundred and thirty years later.

The invasions and alarms of the American Revolution did little or nothing to hinder exploration. While Quebec was under siege, Thomas Frobisher–one of the three Yorkshire Frobishers in the Canadian fur trade–was tracing the one thousand-mile Churchill River to its headwaters close to the present Alberta-Saskatchewan boundary line. Peter Pond, the Connecticut Yankee freelancing out of Detroit, was deep in the Athabaska country, drawing the rough maps that would lead a dozen others farther into that fascinating web of lakes and rivers.

equal to the task

A curly-haired young man from the Hebridean island of Lewis, apprenticed to one of the Montreal firms that merged into the North West Company, took to the West. Alexander Mackenzie's father and uncle were officers in John Johnson's Loyalist regiment, the "Royal Greens," during the War of Independence. The boy Alex, then aged thirteen, was sent for safety and schooling to Montreal where many Scots were already well established as merchants. At fifteen, he was clerking in a fur warehouse on the Montreal waterfront.

Mackenzie was cast in the mould of the times. He stood only five-feet-five inches, stocky, dark, intense, with, in his own words, "a constitution and frame of body equal to the most arduous undertakings." Spending the winter of 1787-1788 with Pond, Mackenzie learned that Lake Athabaska drained northwards by the Slave River into Great Slave Lake and that it, in turn, discharged into other rivers in search of the sea.

Could this be the fabled route to the Pacific?

Unlike those before him, Mackenzie set about putting the question to the test. Such an enterprise was not for doubters. Mackenzie later wrote: "I not only contemplated the practicability of penetrating across the continent, but was confident in my qualifications to undertake the perilous enterprise."

On June 3, 1789, with three canoes, he set out

60

from Lake Athabaska with a copy of Pond's map in his pocket. He also packed some gold guineas to buy stores from the Russians whom he expected to meet in Alaska. His companions were four *Canadien* canoemen, a German, an Indian known as the English Chief, a group of Indian hunters and four native women.

After battling late ice and heavy rains, they entered Great Slave Lake which was still mostly frozen over. After a time-consuming, shore-hugging journey around the vast expanse, they found the western exit – half a mile wide. Mackenzie noted: "We could observe a vast many fish in the water & the place was almost covered with wildfowl, swan, geese & several kinds of ducks."

As the expedition was swept along, almost directly westwards into unknown territory, Mackenzie must have begun to think he had found the Oregon, the "Great River of the West," sought since the days of Champlain. He could see a range of snow-capped peaks before him and he wondered what kind of a gorge would open to allow the river to pass. The canoes hoisted a short sail whenever feasible and covered as much as one hundred miles in a day.

always northward

Soon, however, the mile-wide mainstream began to swing northwards. Day after day Mackenzie pressed his voyageurs forward, excited by the ease of navigation but depressed by the continuing northerly direction. The mountain barrier remained unbroken on his left hand.

On July 5 (in that high latitude the sun had risen at 1:53 A.M.) the explorers surprised a small band of Dogrib and Slave Indians. Pathetically poor, the men were naked, with tattoo'ed cheeks and pierced noses. They warned Mackenzie of fearsome dangers ahead, in the lands of their traditional enemies the Eskimo. Gifts of a knife, axe

The Journey of Samuel Hearne

On November 6, 1769, a twenty-six-year-old ex-sailor named Samuel Hearne left the HBC's Prince of Wales Fort on the western shore of Hudson Bay, in search of some mythical mountain range of copper toward the northwest. Inexperienced and murderous guides almost cost him his life on this and a second attempt. In September, 1770, he met the Chipewyan chief Matonabbee, and after a trek of 1,000 miles (mostly on foot), starvation, frostbite and violence, Hearne and his party reached the mouth of the Coppermine. They found little copper and returned home.

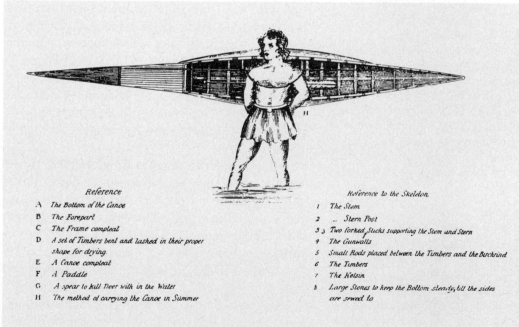

Reference		Reference to the Skeleton	
A	The Bottom of the Canoe	1	The Stem
B	The Forepart	2	Stern Post
C	The Frame compleat	3 3	Two forked Sticks supporting the Stem and Stern
D	A set of Timbers bent and lashed in their proper shape for drying	4	The Gunwalls
E	A Canoe compleat	5	Small Rods placed between the Timbers and the Birchrind
F	A Paddle	6	The Timbers
G	A spear to kill Deer with in the Water	7	The Kelsin
H	The method of carrying the Canoe in Summer	8	Large Stones to keep the Bottom steady, till the sides are sewed to

Although Hearne failed to locate the copperfields of the Northwest and concluded that the "Northwest Passage" did not exist, he learned the essentials of survival from his guide. Before braving the Barrens, they gathered bark and wood for building canoes and shelter.

**Alexander Mackenzie
A Hero Who Failed**

His first view of business was at the age of 12, at the office of his uncle, "Ready Money John," in New York in 1774. At the peak of his success in the fur trade, he was one of the top partners in the North West Company. But when he died in 1820, his wife had to sue to get the money to pay creditors. However, business was not the only obsession in Mackenzie's life. The other was exploration. At 21, he was a "wintering partner" in the west; three years later became the head of the Lake Athabaska region; and in 1789 made the first voyage downriver to the Arctic Ocean. In 1793, he made a three-month journey across the mountain barrier to the Pacific, the first to cross Canada. Nevertheless, Mackenzie's findings did not bring him fame or fortune. His own fur company (known as the XY Company) was bought out by the Nor'Westers, and he returned to Scotland, where he died in 1820.

and kettle persuaded one brave to accompany the Europeans as guide.

A week later, in a wide delta of marshy islands, Mackenzie climbed a rise and saw icefields before him. The rise and fall of a salt tide had been measured. "It is evident these waters must empty themselves into the Northern Ocean," he wrote. At 69° 14' North, he erected a claim post in the permafrost of Whale Island, and then began the gruelling upstream return journey on his "River of Disappointment."

road to nowhere

Mackenzie had traced one of the world's greatest rivers – draining seven hundred thousand square miles – and had become the second European to reach the Arctic coast of Canada overland. His river was to become the main highway of the Northwest, navigable by sizeable craft for almost its entire length. He had seen evidence of petroleum deposits and seams of combustible coal – hints of a mineral wealth then unimaginable. But it was not beaver country, and it did not lead to the Pacific. To the flint-eyed North West Company directors in Montreal, it was just a splendid road to nowhere.

Alex Mackenzie was far from crushed. He remembered the two large rivers which flowed out of the mountainous West: one (the Peace) joined the Slave just above Lake Athabaska, and the other (the Liard) entered "Mackenzie's River" at its northward bend. Did one of these hold the golden key to the Pacific? He was still determined to find out.

During the next two winters, Mackenzie hungrily gathered every scrap of knowledge or rumour from the Indians coming out of the West. He decided that the Peace – a mile wide where it rushed into the Slave – offered the best bet. But first he went to Britain on leave in 1791, primarily to improve his knowledge of astronomy and navigation. He knew, that to convince the scientific experts, the explorer had to fix his geographical positions exactly.

Soon after dawn on May 9, 1793, at a forward base on the Peace near where it was joined by the Smoky, Mackenzie was at the riverbank making a last-minute check of equipment for his second attempt to reach the Pacific. He had carefully packed his new sextant, compass, telescope and pocket chronometer. Comparing his position with Captain Cook's observations in Queen Charlotte Sound, he knew he was about five hundred miles from the coast.

The whole party embarked in a single custom-made *canot de maître*, twenty-five feet long, fifty-seven inches in the beam, twenty-six inches in depth. Made of birchbark sheets over ribs of ash, cedar-fibre stitching sealed with heated pine pitch, it could carry ten men and three thousand pounds of freight – and yet was light enough to be either towed by manpower or carried over portages. The cargo included pemmican and other foods, guns, ammunition, kegs of rum and presents for the Indian bands they expected to encounter.

a week's hard paddling

Mackenzie's second-in-command was another Scot, Alexander Mackay. There were two Indians (one called The Crab) and six voyageurs: Jacques Beaucham, François Beaulieux, Baptiste Bisson, François Courtois, Charles Ducette and Joseph Landry. The last-named pair had been with Mackenzie on his river run to the Beaufort Sea four years earlier.

The Rockies rose to view after a week's hard paddling, and by May 22 Mackenzie was in the canyon where the river burst through the mountains. Along one spectacular stretch, the granite walls reared three hundred feet, the river losing all resemblance to its name. "It was awful to behold with what infinite force the water drives against the rocks," Mackenzie wrote.

Within the mountains, the river split into northern and southern streams. As advised, Mackenzie took the South Fork (it was to be called the Parsnip). This soon turned into a rocky cascade, and every mile was a back-breaker. When the two Scots climbed a ridge to scout the going ahead, they were appalled at the fantastic jumble of mountains and canyons that surrounded them. Mackenzie said nothing to his grumbling crew, except "Forward."

across the divide

On June 12, after manhandling canoe and stores across yet another ridge, the expedition stumbled upon a small clear lake. The elevation was 2,650 feet. The outlet stream flowed to the south-west! Mackenzie knew he had crossed the divide; from here, all waters ran to the Pacific.

If anything, the going got tougher. Flash floods, splintered uprooted trees, waterfalls, marshes . . . the canoemen grew more sullen. Guided by Sekani and Carrier Indians—and occasionally the target of arrows—the party launched into a wide, fast river which Mackenzie figured had to be the Columbia.

Completing a wide swing around the northern end of a high range, the new river (we know it as the Fraser) began to race almost due south. This did not suit Mackenzie's plan. He knew the ocean now lay only some six degrees longitude to the west. He had provisions for only thirty days, and the hunting was poor. A Shuswap brave warned with birchbark drawings of many cataracts ahead.

Making the kind of decision that set explorers aside from other men, Mackenzie turned back on June 21, fighting his way upstream for some sixty miles to where he had noted a strong stream join-ing from the west. This was the Blackwater, which Mackenzie called the West Road River. Carriers assured him that this tributary led to their own trading trail to the coast, and they showed manufactured trinkets and knives as evidence of their commerce.

This river quickly took the party deep into the forested highlands, and Mackenzie slept beside the Indian guide in case he should try to slip away. Drenching cold rain further lowered the spirits of the voyageurs, and the Scots thought it wise to keep pouring liberal tots of rum.

When the little river dropped and twisted impossibly, Mackenzie ordered the canoe to be hidden under brush with a cache of pemmican, wild rice and corn. Making up ninety-pound backpacks for his men—the Indians, used to travelling light, complained bitterly when given forty-pound ones—Mackenzie led his expedition onwards by foot on July 4, over a clearly defined trail. That night they were received hospitably in an Indian camp where metal implements (and an English half-penny) indicated previous contact with white men.

salt water — at last

News of their coming was now flashed ahead by forest telegraph and reception parties were waiting. The travellers were passed over the watershed from camp to camp, and Mackenzie noted with satisfaction that the waters of a new river (the Dean) flowed west.

Here, the river was navigable and a large dugout canoe was exchanged for small trade items. In it Mackenzie and his men ran down to salt water at the head of Dean Channel, a narrow inlet of the ocean, on July 20.

The continent had been crossed by land for the first time! Soon Mackenzie could see the expanse of the Pacific before him. Just seven weeks earlier, one of Captain George Vancouver's longboats had

VOYAGES

D'ALEX.ᴰᴿᴱ MACKENZIE

DANS L'INTÉRIEUR

D E

L'AMÉRIQUE SEPTENTRIONALE,

FAITS en 1789, 1792 et 1793;

Le 1.ᵉʳ, de Montréal au fort Chipiouyan et à la mer Glaciale; Le 2.ᵐᵉ, du fort Chipiouyan jusqu'aux bords de l'Océan pacifique.

PRÉCÉDÉS d'un Tableau historique et politique sur le commerce des Pelleteries, dans le Canada.

TRADUITS DE L'ANGLAIS,

PAR J. CASTÉRA,

AVEC des Notes et un Itinéraire, tirés en partie des papiers du vice-amiral BOUGAINVILLE.

TOME PREMIER.

PARIS,

DENTU, Imprimeur-Libraire, Palais du Tribunat, galeries de bois, n.º 240.

AN X. — 1802.

This copy of Alexander Mackenzie's Voyages *was read by Napoleon during his exile on St. Helena, and may have inspired the emperor's dream of regaining Canada for France.*

been in that same inlet, charting the coastline from the sea.

Mackenzie's achievement did not cease there. He took all his men back to Lake Athabaska without loss or serious injury. Then he returned to the east, stopping off in Upper Canada to report his success first to Lieutenant-Governor Simcoe and then to the fur trade moguls in Montreal. Once again, those gentlemen were not much impressed; Mackenzie's route was obviously far too rugged to serve as a trade road in a business already hard-pressed by operating costs.

Before his death from Bright's disease at fifty-six, Mackenzie wrote a world best-seller, the account of his Canadian explorations. He became the leading celebrity of the fur trade and was knighted in 1802 by George III. When Captains Lewis and Clark, with all the power and support of the United States Army behind them, crossed the continent from St. Louis to the Columbia mouth in 1805, Mackenzie knew that American claims to the Pacific must follow. He argued strongly for the establishment of visible British power along that coast forty years before the first log fort was erected on Vancouver's Island.

The last large secrets of the Cordillera were painstakingly unravelled by another Briton of humble beginnings who became a major character in the exploration drama. David Thompson joined the Hudson's Bay Company as a clerk at age fourteen in 1784. In his late twenties he switched to the North West Company. When he left the West in 1812, he had covered about fifty-six thousand miles by canoe, dogsled, on horseback and on foot.

Thompson discovered the source of the Mississippi in the swamps of northern Minnesota. He was the first European to trace the Columbia, from its birth ponds in the Canadian Rockies some eleven hundred and fifty miles to its ocean outfall.

The Hudson's Bay Company's King George *sets sail from Gravesend, England, en route to the company's posts in Canada. Goods from overseas usually reached the fur forts once a year, and although ships on the Hudson Bay run were built to withstand the force of ice floes, skippers needed skill to avoid the uncharted hazards of the Bay trip.*

With linking lakes and rivers this gave the Canadian fur trade its long-sought route to the Pacific.

It was May 1807 when Thompson first penetrated the eastern ranges of the Rockies, using the five thousand foot Howse Pass (west of today's Rocky Mountain House). This route led him to Blaeberry Creek, a primary source of the Columbia. That same year, Simon Fraser, having followed Mackenzie's route into the mountains farther north, was preparing for his own epic river run to the sea. Fraser named the Thompson River for his colleague, although Thompson never saw that particular system. Mackenzie and Fraser both mistakenly believed they were on the Columbia.

The confusion existed for several more years over the main waterways of that mysterious mountain world. Actually, the Fraser and the Columbia ran almost parallel within the Cordillera, like two giant fish hooks lying one within the other. Both flowed *north* before swinging into their southerly courses.

Thompson finally solved the conundrum of the Columbia in 1811. Four years had elapsed since the time, with his *Métis* wife Charlotte and three small children, he had first stood at Blaeberry Creek, scribbling in one of his voluminous notebooks:

We came to a little rill whose current descends to the Pacific Ocean. May God in his mercy give me to see where its waters flow into the ocean, and return in safety.

When Thompson's party of nine did reach the Columbia mouth in his cedar-plank boat with the Union Jack flapping at the stern, they found the Stars and Stripes waving over Fort Astoria. The log stockade of the Pacific Fur Company had been built four months earlier. The American presence was established in "the Oregon" by land and by sea, and it would endure.

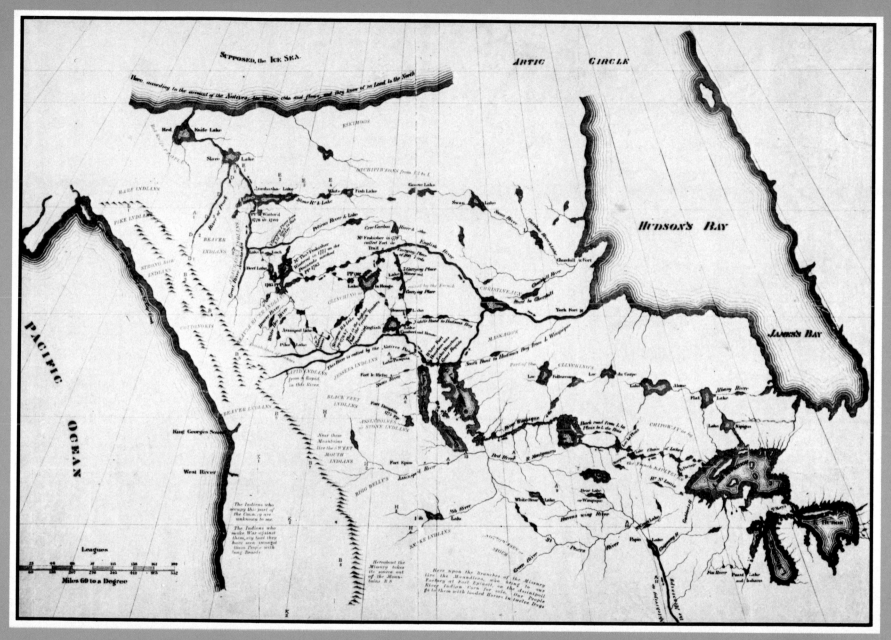

If Peter Pond's 1785 map of Canada's Northwest seems strange in its detail and markings, there was a good deal of method to his madness. Working for the North West Company, Pond's intention was to give the impression that his firm was vigorously exploring the territory, and thereby enlist government support for the company's claims. For example, his "Great River Araubaska" (the Mackenzie) was not followed to its mouth until four years later. Pond no doubt made his sketch from descriptions given him by the Athapaskans, whom he calls "Sweet Mouth Indians." The map is full of similar faux pas: "Hearabouts the Missury takes its source"; "endless Ice Sea"; and so on. Whether Pond's map of these unseen lands convinced anyone that the Nor'Westers were "on the spot" is unlikely. In 1787, he was forced to retire after being linked to two murders, and a new crop of explorers set to work filling in his blanks.

Changing Cultures

For over two hundred years, the Indian tribes of the East had felt the steady encroachment of the white man's way of life, but while firebrands like Pontiac and Neolin, "The Prophet," warned against alliances with the English and the Americans, most Indians accepted the outcomes of wars and struck new bargains with traders, soldiers and land agents.

Nicholas Vincent Iswanhonhi, a chief of the Hurons, posed for this portrait in a mixture of finery when he was presented at Court to King George III.

Both the Protestant and Catholic churches recruited native missionaries to spread the Gospel. Above, Omai carries the stool from which he preached.

It is obvious from this painting that artist Thomas Davies (see also pages 22-23) was much better at painting landscapes than people. However, his 1788 view of this encampment opposite Quebec clearly shows the influence of commerce. Woven cloth, guns, metal implements and brandy were high-value items of trade.

Even though the main subject of this portrait by Benjamin West is the British Superintendent of Indian Affairs, Guy Johnson, the real focus of the painting is the figure in the background — the Mohawk chief Joseph Brant (Tyendinaga). Of all the paintings done in the period, no work summarizes the intricate relationship between the Iroquois and British as this does: Guy Johnson was the nephew of William Johnson, and succeeded him as Superintendent of Indian Affairs in 1774; Brant was the brother of William Johnson's third wife, Molly. First through the fur trade, then defence alliances, land deals, intermarriages and commissions, the Johnsons and the Brants secured a peace between most of the Iroquois and the British that lasted for generations. In part it was this alliance that maintained the British toehold in North America from New France's fall to the end of America's revolution.

CHAPTER SIX

Collision of Cultures

*Englishmen, although you have conquered
the French, you have not conquered us . . .
We are not your slaves.*

Chief of the Chippewa, 1763

Fifty chieftains, all in a show of plumage and paint, wrapped in their ceremonial blankets, stamped into the council chamber within the stockaded British fort at Detroit. Their leader, the forty-three-year-old Pontiac, chief of the Confederacy of the Three Fires, solemnly returned the greeting of Major Henry Gladwin, commander of the 120-man Redcoat garrison. The Indians had asked for a parley to discuss important matters. It was May 7, 1763.

Nearly three years had passed since the surrender at Montreal brought British rule to Canada. The Indians, whether they knew it or not, were now wards of the Crown. The intention of the new King's ministers to keep settlers out of the central heartland of the continent was already known—and would be officially proclaimed later in the year. But the chiefs knew from experience that it would take more than words to keep the land-hungry settlers of the Thirteen Colonies out of the fertile valleys of the Ohio and Mississippi. They feared that the intruders would be joined by more of the same determined breed now streaming from the northeast into the hunting grounds below the Great Lakes.

Seeing clearly the eventual threat to all Indian life, the leaders of the mid-western tribes were agreed on desperate means.

The nations of the Iroquoian Confederacy had stayed loyal to their British allies throughout the Seven Years' War, and, under the guidance of the Johnson family of the Mohawk Valley, still remained staunch—all except the Seneca, whose territory around the Niagara Peninsula was already eroded. For a year or more, the Seneca had been trying to win the agreement of their former traditional enemies—the Ojibwa, Potawatamis, Delawares, Ottawas, Miamis, Shawnees, Fox, Wyandots, Kickapoos and others—for a mass rising against the British western frontier. Leadership had fallen to Pontiac, the tough, handsome chief of the Ottawas who had first challenged the approach of the British from Lake Erie in the winter of 1760.

In the Detroit council chamber, when the usual elaborate courtesies were over, Pontiac expressed his indignation over the presence of a row of armed Redcoats around the room. Did the great father king not trust his Indian children? For an answer, Gladwin pulled aside the blanket of a nearby chief, revealing a musket held under his armpit. All the Indians carried concealed arms—as did the braves and squaws who had been filtering into the compound since dawn, pretending to trade. A signal for the slaughter of every white

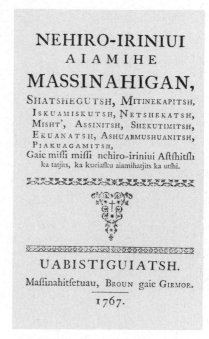

This prayerbook and catechism, one of the first printed, was translated into the Montagnais dialect by the Jesuit Jean-Baptiste La Brosse.

British Indian Affairs Department officers wore these natty green outfits and tophats as their uniform. Informal land deals and outright chicanery were discouraged by proclamation in 1763.

man had been arranged: the handing over of a wampum belt signifying eternal friendship.

The British had been tipped off well in advance. The line of Redcoats with primed guns was more than enough to abort the massacre. Gladwin knew that no Indian believed attack against a prepared enemy to be sensible, even though Pontiac had fifteen hundred armed men in the Detroit villages and surrounding woods.

reign of terror

Both leaders instantly donned the masks of diplomacy. Gladwin reiterated the British offer of friendship and trade – as long as the tribes merited the King's favour – and handed out gifts to help the chiefs save face. Pontiac withdrew without violence.

Detroit was at the bottleneck of the western route through the lakes and for this reason had been chosen for the first move against the British-occupied forts. Once clear of the fort and its covering cannons, Pontiac launched a siege, and a reign of terror began along the river and on the shores of the basin now known as Lake St. Clair.

Few of the other mid-western forts – most of them held by mere handfuls of Redcoats and traders – were as lucky or well-officered as Detroit. As the summer advanced, the posts at Sandusky, St. Joseph, Miami, Ouaitenon, Venango, Le Boeuf and Presqu'Isle all fell to Pontiac's men, some through treacherous ruses. Most of the garrisons were butchered. At Mackinac, the soldiers were lured out of their fort on June 2 to watch a friendly game of lacrosse. Once they were outside, the Indians dropped their sticks and picked up their tomahawks. Only Fort Pitt (now Pittsburgh, Pennsylvannia) stood safely.

About a thousand Europeans were established as farmers or traders along the Detroit corridor. The great majority were French, and these went about their chores circumspectly knowing that Pontiac was not after their blood. The English had been efficiently fingered. James Fisher and his young wife were scalped at Belle Isle and their children taken to an unknown fate. A supply convoy for Niagara was ambushed and several dozen men were burned at the stake where the city of Windsor now stands. An Englishwoman was seized only half a mile from the fort and murdered in cold blood along with her two young sons.

Suicidal frontal assault never appealed to Indian tacticians and although Pontiac sent six hundred men to storm Fort Detroit, not one actually reached the palisades. The resolute Gladwin, maintaining tight discipline throughout, with water stored against fire hazard, his cannons hurling grape shot at any living target, weathered the six-month siege until, finally, the chiefs quarrelled among themselves and the backwoods army melted away. Elsewhere the war flamed and flickered until, at Oswego on Lake Ontario in July, 1766, Pontiac buried the hatchet before William Johnson.

desperate, bloody campaigns

The Pontiac rebellion during its three years took the lives of about five hundred British soldiers – a heavier cost than was paid for the capture of Quebec. The loss of life among frontier settlers, men, women and children, was estimated at two thousand. Pontiac himself was tomahawked two years after the peace near the junction of the Mississippi and the Missouri. The mini-war that bears his name was not the first and would not be the last of the desperate but doomed Indian campaigns to turn back the advance of the European into North America.

The Iroquois had harried the French for nearly a century, pinning their settlers into the lower St. Lawrence. In New England, the Pequots and the Narragansetts fought the Puritans. During the American Revolution – partly triggered by the British decision to reserve the land over the Appalachians for the Indians – the same tribes that had fought the British under Pontiac now fought *for* the British against the rebelling colonists. There may have been some shifts in the European alignments, but to the Indian the nature of the threat was unchanged. The year 1777 became known as "the year of the bloody sevens", a year of guerilla warfare waged by the Indians (sometimes under Canadian officers) on the scattered settlements in the watershed of the Ohio.

no guarantee of peace

Even after the formal peace of 1783, Indians continued to raid the U.S. frontier. When General Washington sent an army to the Wabash in 1791, it was thrashed by an alliance of the Shawnees and the Miamis; the Americans lost 632 killed and 264 wounded, their worst single military disaster to that time. This cohesion of the mid-western tribes, usually splintered and quarreling, was ascribed to the statesmanship of Joseph Brant, the Iroquois leader Tyendinaga, now settling his people on their land grants north of Lake Erie. Brant accepted an invitation to Philadelphia in 1792 where he was offered honours and wealth if he would guarantee peace on the Ohio. He accepted nothing and promised only that he would counsel an end to hostilities. But his own people grew suspicious of his motives – and so did Lieutenant-Governor Simcoe of Upper Canada.

Simcoe had rebuilt Fort Miami at the rapids on the Maumee River south of Lake Erie, and it was still being held for Britain when General Anthony Wayne advanced with a well-trained army. At nearby Fallen Timbers, the American cavalry and sharpshooters met a disorganized amalgam of seven tribes. The Indians were badly beaten on the

William Johnson
Colonel of the Six Nations

When the war between England and France came to an end, so did the free flow of rum, guns and presents to the Indians, and it became the job of William Johnson to enforce the unpopular new policy. As the Superintendent of Indian Affairs since 1755, Johnson knew a great deal about the delicate balance in trade between whites and natives. He had settled in the Mohawk Valley in 1738 as a trader, and quickly earned the respect and confidence of the Iroquois. In 1746, he was named "Colonel of the Six Nations," and during the war with France led British and Indian forces at Lake George and Niagara. By his third wife, Molly Brant, he had eight children, and it was probably by this mixed-marriage that he was able to keep the Iroquois at peace throughout the 1763-66 uprisings.

**Obwandiyag
Pontiac of the Three Fires**

In 1763, when fighting erupted on the western frontier, war with the Indians had almost become a way of life for the British colonists. At the centre of this new trouble was the proud and vindictive war chief of the Ottawas, Pontiac. Almost nothing is known about his first 30 years, but he probably fought in French and Indian raids against British posts in the Seven Years' War. From that time, we see him chafing against British rule in the west. Although his call for "all Nations to take up the Hatchet against the English" was ignored by most tribes, over 2,000 whites were killed by his warriors. In 1766, however, Pontiac relented and accepted the terms of peace. Three years later, at Cahokia, Illinois, he was murdered by the nephew of a Peoria Indian chief.

field and slaughtered in retreat. It was the last act of the central Indian empire, and the subsequent defeat of Tecumseh and his allies at Tippecanoe was only a tragic curtain call. All the later Indian wars could end in only one way: defeat and degradation for the still-primitive people who had prospered on the continent for a hundred centuries or more. They were intelligent, stoic, brave in their fashion, endlessly resourceful, spiritual in the deepest sense, but they were caught out of time in a fatal collision of cultures.

complex culture unfolds

Only one facet of the complex Indian social fabric was revealed in their warfare. Much more important were their richly varied life-styles, skills, cosmology and traditions slowly being disclosed to the outside world. As the British grasp of Canada widened from coast to coast, at the close of the 18th century, a fascinating social mosiac was uncovered.

Scattered very thinly as they were, sometimes ignorant of the very existence of other native "nations", Indians were found in every region and their societies reflected the environments in which they were shaped. Everywhere, Indian life was inspired and disciplined by naturalistic faiths in which men were linked to all other living things. Each tree, flower, bird, animal and fish had its separate spirit, and this was true in a broader sense of the sun, the moon, lightning and thunder, the rivers and of mother earth herself.

Almost every Indian possessed amulets, charms, "medicine" bags of herbs or bones to be worn on the person; this ritual equipment was involved in the communion with the spirits. Certain robes and hair styles, body paint and ornaments, including nose and ear rings, had special significance. If the Ojibwa saw a meteor, they thought war must be near. The Ottawas believed the flickering aurora in the northern sky was a dance by the legions of the dead. Their dances that seemed little more than monotonous shuffling and stamping to the European had each its meaning, often a religious one. In an illiterate society, there was a form of "writing" in the language of ritual, endlessly repeated, embroidered and deepened from one generation to the next.

In most Indian nations each tribe, clan or band had its *shaman*, the "medicine man" who claimed contact with the spirit world . . . not so far removed perhaps, from the Christian prelate at his prayers. The *shaman* appeared in many costumes and in many roles. He was doctor, dentist and counsellor. He could appeal to the gods for help for an individual or for the whole tribe, asking for many sons, heavy crops, good hunting or success in war. He could cast a spell to bring disaster to an enemy.

In the clash of concepts between the red man and the white man nothing was more central than those surrounding ownership of the land. Even the most honourable of the early arrivals, in attempting the purchase of land, were met with mistrust and hostility. No Indian, individual or tribe, owned land in the sense understood by the European. Like the air and the water, the land was free to all.

buying Mother earth

True, a band or a tribe claimed rights over certain territory, but as the supply of game waned or the land was worked out by cropping, the tribe would migrate. Such a cycle of mass movement could take decades. Inter-tribal conflicts could empty areas measured in hundreds of square miles. When a white man struck an agreement with the apparent local Indian authority, the buyer could later be faced with conflicting claims from other native groups who had, at the time, merely been absent on the cycle of their migrations.

The Allies

This cartoon savagely satirizes the 1777 alliance between Britain and the very Indian tribes she had fought in the uprisings of 1763 to 1766. Called the "year of the bloody sevens," 1777 saw a gruesome war on American settlements along the Ohio watershed, waged by Indian tribes fearful of U.S. expansion. The creator of this piece, clearly in sympathy with the plight of American settlers on the frontier, must have patterned the cartoon after earlier ones drawn by British artists two decades earlier during the Seven Years' War. At that time, British settlers were shown as victims of a French-Indian conspiracy.

The Six Nations

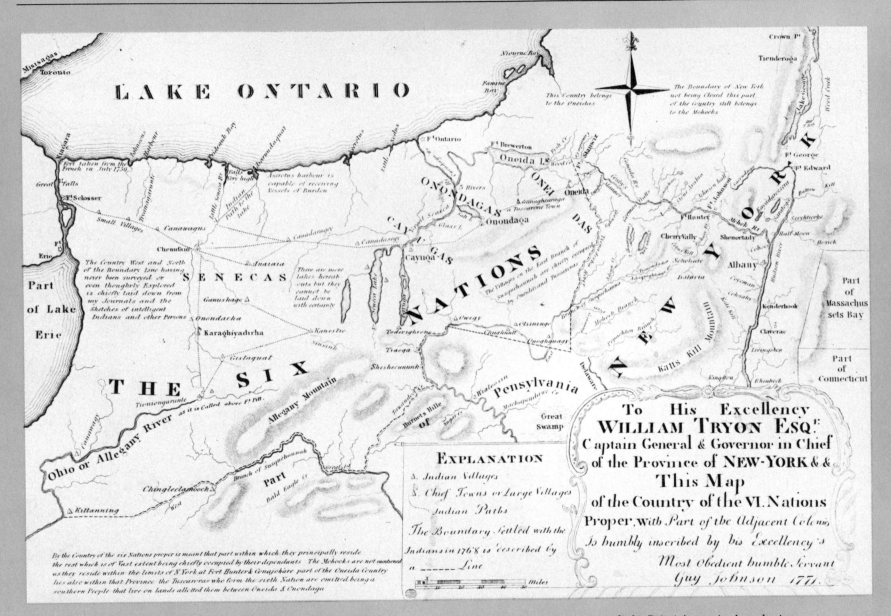

Ironically, the Iroquois Confederacy, at the high point of its civilization at the middle of the 18th century, was split by Britain's war in the colonies. The Tuscarora and the Oneida sided with the Thirteen Colonies, and the Six Nations, for long allied to England, was divided by new conflicts of loyalties.

Once British rule was firmly established, the private purchase of property from the natives was forbidden, but, although the treaties under which the Crown took formal possession of the land were detailed in millions of words over a hundred years, the full meaning of the Indian's relationship with the earth-mother could never be reduced to paper.

Without Indian hospitality and hunting lore, the European penetration would have been a much more difficult task. As they came to understand something of life in other lands, the Indian was shocked to learn that some people might go short of food while others had plenty. Within the tribal family, or with the friendly stranger, the sharing of food was unquestioned routine. Many settlers struggling to hack an existence out of the Canadian bush after the American Revolution had reason to bless the Indian who came to the cabin door offering salmon, perch and pike, the meat of hare, deer, bear, moose, beaver tail and seasonal wildfowl.

sharing the bounty

Indian corn (maize), beans and pumpkins, domesticated and developed in the New World over some five thousand years, were readily adopted by the pioneers. Berries and other wild fruits unknown in Europe were added to the diet. In the meticulous diary she kept during her four years (1792-1796) in Upper Canada, Elizabeth Simcoe frequently recorded gifts and purchases from the Indians.

Tuesday, Aug. 13, 1793: *An Indian named Wable Casigo supplies us with salmon, which the rivers and creeks on this shore (Toronto Bay) abound with . . . They are best in the month of June.*

Sunday, April 3, 1796: *Some Indians brought maple sugar to sell in birchbark baskets. I gave three dollars for thirty pounds.*

Monday, April 4, 1796: *Some Indians brought some excellent wild geese from Lake Simcoe, and several kinds of ducks, which were very pretty as well as very good. The wild rice off which they feed makes them so much better than wild ducks in England.*

Although firearms were widely distributed among the Indian hunters of the eastern woodlands, difficulties of repair and irregular supply of shot and powder kept the old hunting techniques in use. The pit, the snare and the deadfall were the principal tools, and the arrow had by no means been discarded. A skilful hunter could stalk deer at the forest edges until the beast was within sure range.

deadfalls, snares and fire

The snare was a loop of sinew or thin rope of rawhide, tied to a sapling bent to form a natural spring. The trapped animal released a simple trigger and was hanged when the tree sprang upright. A deadfall operated when the animal, in pulling at a bait, knocked away a thin stick that supported a heavy tree trunk. Birds were seized on the nest at night, and in winter a hunter on rawhide snowshoes could run down a deer or moose.

One of the most ingenious devices was the setting of a bent blade in a ball of frozen fat. Tossed in the path of bear or wolf, the lethal tidbit would open in the stomach of the prey.

Some of the earliest French and English traders and travellers wrote about the Indian communal hunting drives and while game remained plentiful, this technique was followed in all regions. The animals were herded by a wide cordon of hunters (including the women and children) and driven into a man-made corral or a gorge where they could be butchered. Smoke was used to flush game from hiding and flaming torches to dazzle the eyes of deer at night. Natural narcotic

FRONTISPEICE

EUROPE, ASIA, AFRICA and AMERICA bringing Intelligence to the GENIUS of the LONDON MAGAZINE.

In 1778 the date of this issue of The London Magazine, or Gentleman's Monthly Intelligencer, North America wasn't the only continent of concern to the Colonial Office. Natives from the far-flung reaches of the Empire were often brought to London (usually as curiosities) to shed some light on doings abroad.

John Lambert chronicled his travels in Canada in three volumes in 1814, illustrating his diary with sketches such as this one titled "An Indian and his Squaw." Though the drawing is crude and uncomplimentary, it documents one of the sad truths of the period. By the century's end liquor, the gun trade and epidemics of smallpox (the worst in 1781-82) had already begun to destroy the traditions of many Indian tribes.

substances—such as that extracted from the roots of the walnut tree—were released into fresh water pools to aid in fishing.

Indian taboos and forbidden practices relating to the eating of game fascinated the educated among the settlers but merely puzzled or angered the majority of whites. Writing about a feast of bear meat, Mrs. Simcoe noted that all of the meat had to be eaten at the one sitting, this requiring some gorging by the diners. (She didn't like the taste herself.) The bear's head was always presented to the chief. The bear was an honoured spirit and must not be insulted in any way. Bear meat could not be brought into a tipi through the same doorway used by women. Among the Micmacs of the Atlantic coastal areas, a hunter would not eat roast porcupine; he believed that if he did he would be slowed down to the pace of that ponderous beast. The bones of the beaver must not be thrown into rivers.

Misunderstanding of Indian sexual customs led to the creation of stubborn myths about the promiscuity of native women. The vague Christian associations between chastity, monogamy and religion had no place in the older Indian societies. There was no tradition of romantic love. Polygamy was the norm in most tribes—were the excess women to be left to starve? A good hunter would generously take several sisters as wives—they were less likely to quarrel than strangers.

Sexual gratification was everywhere thought not only normal but healthy. In some societies wives were loaned freely to tribal brothers, or even strangers. Among the Iroquois, for example, problems of parenthood did not arise: all children belonged solely to the women, who also owned all tribal property and equipment.

Pre-marital sex was usually encouraged, as a form of trial marriage. How could a union be happy and fruitful if the partners were mis-matched? Divorce could be as simple as the wife placing her husband's possessions outside the door of the hut or tipi. The divorced man would return to his mother and sisters, to be received without any sign of disapproval. These apparently casual relationships caused the sexually inhibited European to misunderstand the very deep bonds of the Indian family.

Indian fabrics were freely adopted or adapted by the pioneers, many of them more suited to the Canadian climate or topography than the garb of the civilized world. For fifty years on the remote frontier, the settler's wife sewed buckskin shirts and trousers, shod her children in moose-hide moccasins, and often used native baskets and bowls to supplement her scanty stock. Mrs. Simcoe's two young children, Sophia and Francis, ate breakfast from Indian bowls hollowed out of birch knots and stained red with a dye made from hemlock bark.

The selfless Indian contribution to the European advance into Canada—as into the lands below the border—could not be seen clearly in these early years. The blood-letting by Pontiac, the frontier raids of the Revolution, tribal participation in the War of 1812—all of these kept the white man's attention focused on the Indian of the warpath, and deepened fears of the tomahawk, the scalping knife and the torture stake.

The tragic inability of the Indian to cope with white man's alcohol, his lack of materialistic ambition (seen as laziness), his unconcern with detail (seen as unreliability)—all of these and other traits led him to turn inward. If the Indian could not be tempted or forced to assimilate, to become "civilized," then he would have to be isolated on lands reserved for him alone. Such a policy was soon to be adopted.

The Irish Chieftain

One of the curious sidelights of trade and exchange between the Europeans and native North Americans was the bestowing of titles and ranks: Indian warriors and chiefs were made officers of the armies, often receiving handsome commissions for their aid in combat; and Indian Affairs Department officers were, in return, made honorary chieftains of tribes with which they negotiated treaties and land deals. It is not unusual then that Sir John Caldwell, Fifth Baronet of Castle Caldwell, County Fermanagh, Ireland, a British officer stationed at Fort Niagara and Detroit in the 1770s, is seen here dressed in all the real and fanciful regalia he could muster for an official portrait. The Ojibwa called him Apatto, or The Runner, and although little is known about Caldwell's dealings with the Indians, it is safe to assume he played a major role in providing fire arms to the Ojibwa in their wars against the Sioux and neighbouring tribes. His dress is as much a sign of the times as his title: the wampum belt testifies of treaties; his puckered-seam mocassins are the traditional Ojibwa footwear; his bird-of-paradise feathers recount feats of bravery; and his copper, brass and steel breast plate, ornaments and weapons boast of European might. Whether chiefs wore ruffled blouses is questionable.

It must have been a strange encounter, when the English artist commissioned for this portrait first saw the Irish baronet cum honorary Ojibwa chief decked out in his unusual finery.

Tyendinaga

His enemies called him "the Monster Brant," whose name was "terrible in every ear. . . ." His Mohawk kinsmen named him Tyendinaga, a warrior who had fought his first battle at the age of 13. And to his British allies he was Captain Joseph Brant, a Loyalist whose grandfather, one of the "Four Indian Kings," had some thirty years before his birth gone to England to negotiate a land treaty for the Iroquois. Joseph Brant was born in 1742 in a village on the Ohio River, and in his youth was adopted as a protégé of his sister Molly's husband, Superintendent of Indian Affairs, William Johnson. He was educated at Moor's Indian Charity School in Connecticut, and before the Revolutionary War, spent some time in England, before leading four of the six Iroquois nations in at least two major victories against the rebel states. When the tide of war turned and the Yankees burned and pillaged their villages, Brant led his people north to the Grand River region near present-day Brantford, Ontario, to lands granted by the government. A devout Christian, Brant spent the years until his death in 1804 translating the Scriptures into the Mohawk dialect. The three portraits (here and page 68) reveal the many sides of his character.

This portrait was painted during Brant's return visit to England after the war. He became a close friend of the Prince of Wales and "a lion of London society."

Superintendent of Indian Affairs (and "Colonel of the Six Nations"), Brant's brother-in-law William Johnson acknowledged the aid of Loyalist Iroquois with land grants and testimonials such as the one above. Under Brant's direction, the Mohawk, Onondaga, Cayuga and Seneca tribes showed "repeated proofs of their Attachment to His Britannic Majesty's Interests."

William Berczy's portrait of Brant is thought to be the most accurate likeness of the great Mohawk leader — a sharp contrast with George Romney's portrayal (left).

Indian hunters and trappers (all carrying guns), and their wives and children gather at this clearing to discuss the terms of barter with a fur company trader.

CHAPTER SEVEN

Great Days of the Fur Trade

*Every intelligent Man saw the poverty that
would follow the destruction of the Beaver,
but there were no Chiefs to controul it.*

David Thompson, 1793

Daybreak at Lachine on Lake St. Louis, the widening of the St. Lawrence just south of Montreal. On this May morning at the turn of the 19th century, mist swirls on the brisk breeze funnelling down the Ottawa Valley. At the wharves fronting the warehouses of the North West Company, the great freight canoes, forty feet long, six feet wide, are already loaded. Each one is stacked with sixty-five ninety-pound packs of trade goods, equipment and provisions. Four tons in all. When the crew of twelve step in, each to his place, only six inches of gunwale shows above water.

Allez! The guide from his place of authority in the bow gives the order. The high painted prow swings out into the stream. The steersman, the only man standing, sets the blade of his long paddle. The middlemen, two on a seat, raise their vermilion-tipped paddles. At a grunt from the guide, all blades slice the water in one blurred stroke. The stately birch and cedar craft, so light that four men can carry it, spurts forward. To the rear three more canoes similarly laden form a convoy.

Ashore, a few early rising clerks and labourers, and two or three sleepy women, raise a brief cheer. A solitary musket shot cracks out. No farewell ceremony. Just the routine departure of a Nor'Wester brigade for Fort William, on the far shore of Lake Superior. Nothing to proclaim that here began one of the most interesting and arduous journeys in the history of overland commerce.

No camel train across Asia Minor moved with the surety and efficiency of the canoe brigades in the great days of the Canadian fur trade. No European coach or wagon could survive a single mile of the route: there were no roads, only rocks, rapids and white water all the way. Yet cargo losses on voyage were as low as one-half of one percent.

The first leg hugged the north shore of Lake St. Louis. The voyageurs, tough, uncomplicated Canadians born to the paddle, often of mixed blood, treated this opening stretch as a regatta. Racing to the Ottawa they would hit a pace of forty, forty-five, even fifty paddle strokes a minute. The traditional garb of blue *capote*, deerskin leggings, gaily hued sash and knitted toque, splashed the pale morning with colour.

As the canoes turned west around the tip of Montreal Island into the Ottawa River (then known as the Grand), the voyageurs' paddle songs echoed across the water and the bells answered from the church of Ste.-Anne-de-Bellevue. This was accepted as the true beginning of the journey. Here Irish poet Thomas Moore in 1804, watching the departure of a fur brigade, wrote his "Canadian Boat Song":

To prepare for shipment, Hudson's Bay Company traders packed their furs into large bales, bound them and stamped the company crest on the metal seal—the best-known logo of the great days of the fur trade.

The Contents of Canot 25

Canot, Nᵒ. 25

2735

N.W.		Ballots de Marchandises, No.
		9. 5. 11. 12. 4. 13. 15. 7. 16. 8. 16.
		33. 36. 10. 12. 35. 40. 11. 43.
		15.
	1	Ballots de Tabac noir,
		– – – – de Tabac en carotes,
		– – – de N. W. Twist,
		– – – de Chaudières évasées,
		– – – de Chaudières de cuivre,
		– – – de Chaudières de fer blanc,
	1	– – – de Jambons,
		– – – de Bajoux,
		Barils de Sel,
		– – – de Graisse,
	2	– – – de Poudre,
		– – – de Sucre blanc,
		– – – de Sucre brun,
	4	– – – de Lard,
	20	– – – de High Wines,
		– – – de Rum,
		– – – d'Esprit,
	2	– – – de Bœuf,
	2	– – – de Beurre,
	2	– – – de Shrub,
	1	– – – de Vin de Port,
		– – – de Vin de Madère,
		– – – de Vin rouge,
		– – – d'Eau de vie de France,
		– – – de Langues,
		– – – de Saucisses,
		– – – d'Orge,
		– – – de Riz,
		– – – de Fromage,
		– – – de Raisins,
		– – – de Figues,
		– – – de Prunes,
	2	Cassettes de Marchandises, No. 266,
	2	Caisses de Fer, No. 10. 21.
	1	– – – de Chapeaux, No. 174.
		– – – de Couteaux, No.
		– – – de Fusils,
	1	– – – de Pièges, 53.
		– – – de Savon,
	1	Maccarons de High Wines,
		– – – – d'Esprit,
		– – – – de Rum,
		– – – – Mêlés,
		Paquets de Fer,
		– – – – d'Acier,
		Sacs de Plomb,
	1	– – – de Balles,
		– – – de Pois,
		– – – de Bled d'Inde d'1¼ minot,
		– – – – – – – de 2 minots,
	1	Cuva

Les noms des hommes, savoir :

Amable Lavallé
Jos Le Tenure
Michel Veillette
Antoine Le Fevre
Jos. A. la Fontaine
Jos. Maheux
J.B. Veilleux
J.B. Clemens
Joachim Tourdain

Vivres, savoir :

8 Sacs de Biscuits,
2 – – – de Pois,
200 livres de Lard,

Les Agres, savoir :

1 Hache,
1 Plat de fer blanc,
1 Voile,
2 Prélats,
5 Lignes de Banc,
1 Chaudière,
1 Alêne,
1 rouleau d'Ecorce,
6 bottes de Wattap,
1 Crémaillière,
12 à 18 livres de Gomme.

Bundles of tobacco, barrels of wine and liquor, cases of metal implements and arms and sacks of foodstuffs usually totalling almost 6,000 pounds were itemized on a bill of lading before this crew of nine voyageurs left Lachine on May 6, 1802. The contents of Canot No. 25 was packed into 90-pound bundles for portaging.

*Faintly as tolls the evening chime
Our voices keep tune and our oars keep time.
Soon as the woods on shore look dim,
We'll sing at St. Ann's our parting hymn.
Row, brothers, row, the stream runs fast,
The rapids are near and the daylight's past.*

Skirting around the Ile-Perrot that sits in the mouth of the Ottawa like a cork in a bottle, the voyageurs faced a one thousand-mile ordeal during which they paddled and pulled, shoved and carried their craft and cargo through a maze of rivers, lakes and portages. Speed was most important in keeping rendezvous with the "wintering partners," who were at the same time heading down the rivers of the Northwest towards Thunder Bay with the bales of pelts collected from the Indian hunters. An average day's run was fifty to sixty miles, but a racing crew once covered one hundred miles with six portages.

After a wild carouse at the company's fort at the mouth of the Kaministiquia (the "Kam"), the men from the East packed the season's fur haul into the great canoes and, with a chorus of huzzahs, sprinted away on the return journey to Lachine. They were called "the Comers and Goers," and also *les mangeurs du lard*, or "pork-eaters," – their basic diet was corn and hog grease. Coming and going, amazingly tireless, unfailingly cheerful, they sang their paddle songs:

*A la clair fontaine,
M'en allant promener,
J'ai trouvé l'eau si belle,
Que je m'y suis baigné.
Il y a longtemps que je t'aime,
Jamais je ne t'oublierai.*

The words didn't matter much, often varying from crew to crew. Only the respectable ditties were recorded by the occasional world traveller, songs such as *"Roll, My Ball," "I Have Plucked the*

Beautiful Rose," "The Lovely Lisette," "The First Day of May." Bilingual lady passengers often blushed at obscene parodies of European folk melodies, such as those penned by Pierre Falcon and Willard Wentzel. Knowing that these work songs lightened the tedious labour of paddling, the company paid a bonus to the strong singer.

hub of the fur trade

Famed Fort William was built and named for company chieftain William McGillivray at Thunder Bay after the U.S. border was drawn at the Pigeon River. Here was the nerve centre of the trade, but it was still only a halfway house between the shipping port of Montreal and the far-flung trading posts now reaching beyond Lake Athabaska, into the Rockies and the lower valleys of the Columbia.

Using the Kam as their road towards Rainy Lake, the Lake of the Woods and the river systems of the midwest, the second echelon of the Nor'Wester trading network took over. These were *les hommes du nord*, the proud Northmen, inured to hardship and semi-starvation, often coarse and cruel, living close to the style of those they termed savages, scornful of the soft pork-eaters of the East. Their basic diet was the pemmican—dried buffalo meat mixed with rendered fat and berries—prepared by the *Métis* hunters on the Manitoba plains.

Fort William itself was the most remarkable structure in the immense Northwest, rivalled only by the very different Old World stone bastion of the Hudson's Bay Company on the delta of the Churchill River. Within palisades fifteen feet high where the Kam met the lake, the "lords of the lakes and forests" (as Washington Irving called the Nor'Wester partners) had erected a complex of buildings, storehouses, packing sheds, dormitories, forge and workshops, including the Great Hall (sixty feet long by thirty feet wide) where the executive sat in council and where, in the evenings, dinners and parties were held. A thousand men worked on its construction.

The Great Hall, fronting on to a swept square, was balconied along its length. It could seat two hundred at dinner. And what dinners! Wild duck and geese, lake trout and whitefish, venison, buffalo tongue and hump, beaver tail, fruits and vegetables from the tilled acres around the stockade. And the boozing! These men ate and drank quantities that seem unbelievable. The daily ration of buffalo meat was eight pounds per man. Two whole geese made a single meal for the man from the *pays d'en haut*. West Indies rum, French brandy, Spanish and Portuguese wines were consumed by the barrel. A dozen diners once downed 120 bottles of wine at a sitting.

The roistering went on till dawn. Scottish pipers marched around the hall as the partners and the bourgeoisie jumped on their chairs and "shot the rapids" on tables tilted to the floor. Paunchy self-made men, reliving their youth on Hebridean islands, danced madly in the Highland fling, and, with paddles clamped between their thighs, belted around the hall in mock canoe races that ended in hilarious pile-ups at the corners. Indian and half-breed girls dressed in their beaded finest, waited demurely at beck and call.

the morning after

When the packs of trade goods freighted from Montreal had been sorted and marked by company code for the various inland posts, the Northmen doused their hangovers in the icy water of Superior and began the return journey into the deep wilderness. Their canoes, built for shallower waters and more frequent carries, were about half the size of the *canots du maître*. However, with a crew of four or five, they could still move more

Simon McTavish "Le Marquis"

His partners and competitors had ample reason for dubbing him "Le Marquis" — his domain stretched from Montreal west to the Pacific and north to the Arctic. He was probably the richest man in the whole of Canada. In 1764, he came to America as a boy of 14, and settled in Albany, but within a few years was already travelling far and wide for the fur trade. In 1779, at 29, he put together the original North West Company, which under his direction grew to virtually dominate the fur trade. In business he was known as a domineering blusterer, but in his letters quite a different, generous man emerges. Perhaps the dour Scot in him was tempered by his marriage to Marguerite Chaboillez, daughter of one of the *Canadien* fur traders.

The Fur Trade

The business of the fur trade was a matter of ceremony and ritual respected by factors and Indians alike at most posts. Although the Hudson's Bay Company's "Standard of Trade" was largely lost in the fierce competition from the free-wheeling Montreal "pedlars," Indian suppliers knew well the limits of bargaining. Prefaced by exchanges of presents and pipe smoking, feasting and drinking, the actual transaction was carried on with caution and suspicion: scales and yard-sticks were checked, quality of pelts and goods examined, and records of previous trade consulted. When the bargain was sealed, the furs were piled into huge *canots de maître,* to be paddled to Montreal and shipped to markets in Europe.

The fur company factor's fancy toboggan was a miniature Quebec cariole drawn by a dog team — essential winter transportation.

By 1784, inter-company competition had driven 1725 beaver prices up 100%.

At the trading store, tokens (see page 87) or pelts purchased trade goods.

The Pedlars vs. The Factors

With the fall of New France, the rich fur regions of Canada's Northwest became the focus of interest for English fur trading companies based in Montreal. As the French relinquished their claims and relaxed trade policies took effect, these free-wheeling "pedlars" moved into the territories with astonishing speed. They recruited French-Canadian voyageurs familiar with the Indians and canoe routes; they ignored the age-old territorial claims of the Hudson's Bay Company; they upset the established "standard of trade"; and wooed the HBC's ablest manpower. If the rivalry between the HBC's factors and the "pedlars" was intense, it was keener still among the new firms. Shipments of furs were stolen, Indian trappers were bought off with liquor or bullied into boycotting the competition, and on occasion disputes ended in bloodshed. Between 1775 and 1783, several of these Montreal firms, led by Simon McTavish, Joseph Frobisher, Isaac Todd and James McGill, formed a syndicate called the North West Company, to abate the evils of competition and consolidate their exploration and trade efforts. The poorly-paid Hudson's Bay Company factors, directed from London, were no match for the Nor'Westers. While the Baymen continued to depend on furs brought to their posts on Lake Superior and Hudson Bay, the pedlars moved inland and established posts on Lakes Athabasca and Winnipeg, and on the Red, Saskatchewan and Assiniboine rivers. By doing so they assured themselves of the first choice of the season's pelts and gained the upper hand for a time in the feverish struggle for control.

Daniel Williams Harmon

Chief trader for the NWC in B.C.; father of 14 by a Métis wife; his *Journal* recounts fur trade life.

Joseph Frobisher

One of the first "Pedlars" and a founder of the NWC; Montreal's Beaver Hall was his residence.

than a ton of payload.

All was now speed and efficiency; they had to reach the far terminal of the network before freeze-up. Alexander Mackenzie once logged seventy-two miles in a day against current and head-winds. Then, through the seemingly endless winter, the factors would trade for furs, outbidding or outfighting the competition.

It is a measure of the empty vastness of the country in this era that the fur trade continued and waxed greater through all the conflict that marked the first half century of British rule of Canada. The three years of Pontiac's rising, the eight years of the American War of Independence, the War of 1812-1814, not even the murderous struggle between the fur rivals could stem the single-minded drive to take the coat of every beaver, marten, muskrat, otter, fisher, raccoon, badger, wolverine and fox in the land. The European gentleman had to have his high felt hat and milady her warm muff.

every river and pass

In this pursuit, the adventurers among the Baymen and the Nor'Westers reached out from their bases, tracing every river, threading every pass, until the absolute edges of the country were known and claimed. The search for the dens of the beaver drew the profile of the future nation.

Established by royal charter in the 17th century, the Hudson's Bay Company was already so ancient that wits translated its initials as "Here Before Christ." Its enormous domain of Rupert's Land, from Labrador to the Rockies and dipping south into the Red River Valley, was barely touched during the rebellion of the Thirteen Colonies, except when La Pérouse, demonstrating support for England's foes, raided the main trading posts on Hudson Bay.

At first, the HBC had sat in its several posts

around the rim of Hudson Bay, knowing the Indians had to bring their furs out to trade for kettles, cloth, knives, and firearms. They were finally pushed into chasing business in the interior by the penetration by French traders to the Saskatchewan River. The exploring journeys of Kelsey, Henday, Cocking and other Baymen culminated in the building of Cumberland House (sixty miles north of The Pas, Manitoba), in 1774. It was the first link of a lengthening chain.

the ruthless independents

The following year the opening volley at Lexington cut off the New England colonies from the western trade, and several of the most aggressive traders moved lock, stock and barrel to Montreal and joined the independent operators then competing for the business abandoned by the French in 1760. These "pedlars" (as the Baymen scorned them) stopped at nothing: there was widespread debauchery and cheating of the natives, and several violent deaths.

Simon McTavish, who had left Scotland as a penniless boy of thirteen, finally drew the leading factions into the partnership known from 1783 as the North West Company. By agreeing to share the western trade rather than fighting over it, the pedlars quickly prospered and became serious rivals to the HBC. When McTavish died in 1804, the richest man in Canada, leadership passed to his nephew, William McGillivray. The permanent staff of the company then stood at 1,280, not counting Indians.

The epic journeys of Alexander Mackenzie, Simon Fraser and David Thompson were all, in reality, born of the Nor'Westers' desperate need to find the least expensive river routes across the country. As they had to search ever deeper into the wilderness for abundant pelts, their transport and personnel costs spiralled. The HBC, on the other hand, could bring its goods midway into the continent by cheap ocean freight. Although the Nor'Westers enjoyed three decades of power and riches, their reckless over-expansion and the obstacle of the HBC's Red River farming settlement across their supply route eventually brought them down. In 1821 the surviving partners were absorbed into the Hudson's Bay Company.

Although most of the leading figures were Scots (the records show fifteen McKenzies, fourteen Grants, lots of McDougalls, McGills and Camerons), the indispensable man in the fur trade was the voyageur.

The voyageur was the lineal successor to the *coureur des bois*, the freelance small trader whom the governors of the French regime tried to keep out of the forests, even on pain of death. He was perhaps the first distinctive Canadian. Illiterate, seldom more than five feet tall (big men did not fit easily into canoes), often bandy-legged, swarthy of complexion, he could jog-trot over the portages with two ninety-pound packs; some steel-spined men were known to carry four packs. A Negro, Pierre Bonga, held the record with five . . . a total of 450 pounds.

The vessels they handled so masterfully were all based on the bark canoe, the invention of the Indian tribes of the eastern woodlands. The forest provided all materials, and one could be made with knife alone. The Montreal freighters, the *canots du maître*, were larger and more complicated than anything ever attempted by the Indians. They were built at Trois Rivières during the winter.

The mind-numbing labour of paddling through the daylight hours was broken by pauses, usually once every two hours, when the voyageur opened his *sac-à-feu* and repacked his clay pipe with black tobacco. The rests became known as *pipes*, lasting for about five minutes. Most of the canoemen smoked almost continuously, even when carrying

These Hudson's Bay Company tokens were used as currency in the East Main (EM) district around James Bay. Instead of dollars and cents, the value of the coins was based on beaver pelts or "Made Beaver" – units varying from ⅛ to one pelt. and negotiable at the HBC store.

crushing loads. The distances along the river and lake routes were measured in *pipes*, rather than by miles or leagues.

The cargoes of trade goods were mostly bought in Britain to suit the needs, or desires, of the wilderness tribes as reported by the wintering partners. Apart from the ever-present vermilion (so popular as body paint) and the rum or other "ardent spirits", the canvas-wrapped packs included guns, powder and ammunition, twist tobacco (measured by the fathom), knives, traps and axes, heavy woollen blankets, cloth in blue or scarlet, brass and iron kettles, flints and firesteels, nets and ropes, awls, needles, buckles, combs, beads, rings, and metal crosses. The gross profit realized depended on the distance to the trading post, but four hundred percent was not uncommon.

Although uncouth in many ways – some early journals call them filthy, ignorant, lecherous and superstitious – the voyageurs had an unmistakeable flair, and considerable Gallic charm. "All their talk is about horses, dogs, canoes, women and strong men who can fight a good battle," wrote Daniel Harmon.

tiny mouths to feed

Prostitution was unknown within normal Indian life – and unnecessary. The chiefs had been puzzled but delighted to learn that the fur traders would actually pay for a girl, either for a brief fling at the *rendezvous* or as a more-or-less permanent partner around the inland posts. Efforts were made by all the fur companies to discourage the practice, mainly because of the cost of feeding and housing the native wives and the many halfbreed children. At one time, the North West Company was feeding more than six hundred children.

Not only the voyageurs built up sizeable families: George Simpson, most famous of the HBC governors, sired seven known children by various women he had taken *a la façon du nord*, before he made a legitimate marriage in England. The Nor'Wester Daniel Harmon had ten children with his Elizabeth, "a Canadian's daughter" whom he had "accepted" when she was fourteen. Alexander Henry (The Younger) reported that *Métis* girls were traded as young as ten years old.

slave market in women

The Nor'Westers were generally more commercially minded than their Hudson's Bay rivals. Some of their factors literally ran a slave market in women. The Athabaska factor Archibald McLeod, a member of Montreal's Beaver Club, wrote in his account book:

I gave the Chef de Canard's widow to the amount of twenty-eight plus [beaver skins] and took the Slave woman whom next fall I shall sell for a good price.

James McKenzie at Fort Chipewyan accepted young girls from the Indian hunters in payment of debts and sold them to the highest bidder. But romance could exist in the voyageur's life. Alexander Henry recorded this love story:

One of my men who was much in debt offered me his services as long as he could perform any duty on condition that I clothe him and allow him to take a woman he had fallen in love with . . . This proposal did not surprise me, having seen several people as foolish as he, who would not hesitate to sign an agreement of perpetual bondage on condition of being permitted to have a woman who had struck their fancy.

And the bosses weren't immune, either. "Big" John McDonnell, who still wore a sword, brought his wilderness wife back to Montreal on his retirement and married her legally after a relationship *a la façon du nord* of forty-six years.

Almost every educated traveller in the early 19th century was struck by the open display of wealth and power provided by the fur barons. The American novelist and essayist Washington Irving described some Nor'Wester partners heading for the Fort William *rendezvous*:

They ascended the rivers in great state, like sovereigns making a progress, or rather like Highland chieftains navigating their subject lakes. They were wrapped in rich furs, their huge canoes freighted with every convenience and luxury, and manned by Canadian voyageurs, as obedient as Highland clansmen. They carried up with them cooks and bakers, together with delicacies of every kind, and abundance of choice wines for the banquets which attended this great convocation.

Sometimes one or more of the partners would go to New York on a tour of pleasure and curiosity. On these occasions, there was always a degree of magnificence of the purse about them and a propensity to visit the jewellers for rings, chains, brooches, necklaces, jewelled watches and other costly trinkets, partly for themselves and partly for their female acquaintances.

None of this largesse sifted down to the voyageur, the *engagé*, who, often as not, ended the season in debt to the company. But money mattered little to him: if he had any to jingle, he would throw it away on fiery liquor and the ever-available girls. The company would keep him in rations. The brutish work wore him out early – the average lifespan was around forty years.

A typical voyageur, his best years behind him, once attempted to explain his philosophy:

I spent all my earnings in the enjoyment of pleasure. Now I have not a spare shirt to my back, not a penny to buy one. Yet, if I were young again, I should do the same thing all over again. There is no life as happy as a voyageur's life, no place where a man enjoys such freedom as in the Indian country. Huzza! Huzza! pour le pays sauvage.

From the Continental to the Paris Beau

From the far reaches of Canada's North, beaver pelts travelled thousands of miles to London, Paris and Russia, to carders, combers, felters and furriers, and eventually to the fashion salons of Europe. Every part of the pelt was used – for coats, collars, muffs, mitts, and especially hats. From the middle of the 18th to the middle of the 19th century, military and civilian dandies stayed in vogue with Continentals, Wellingtons and Paris Beaus.

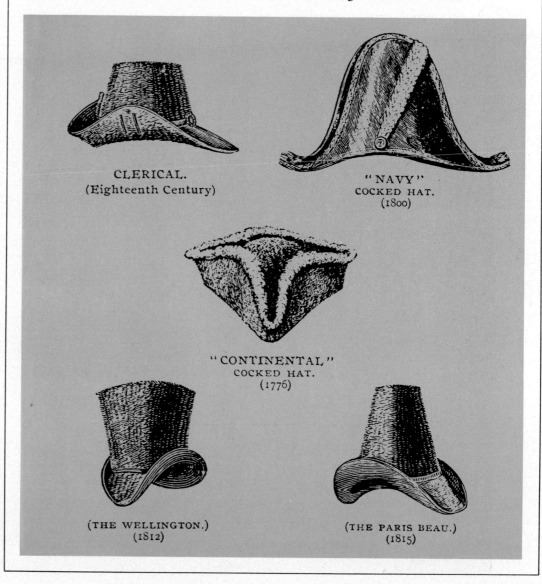

CLERICAL.
(Eighteenth Century)

"NAVY"
COCKED HAT.
(1800)

"CONTINENTAL"
COCKED HAT.
(1776)

(THE WELLINGTON.)
(1812)

(THE PARIS BEAU.)
(1815)

Landfall at Nootka Sound

Captain James Cook's ships *Resolution* and *Discovery* tower above Indian canoes in Nootka Sound during his visit in 1778. Cook had been assigned to explore the north-west coast and locate the "north-west passage" – a strait rumoured to run from the Atlantic to Pacific.

"March 29: We no sooner drew near the inlet, than we found the coast to be inhabited; and at the place where we were first becalmed, three canoes came off to the ship . . . Having come pretty near us, a person in one of the two last stood up, and made a long harangue, inviting us to land. . . ."

"March 30: A great many canoes, filled with the natives, were about the ships all day; and a trade commenced betwixt us and them, which was carried on with the strictest honesty on both sides. The articles which they offered to sale were skins of various animals. . . ." *Diaries of Captain James Cook*

*Although British Columbians have
adopted Captain James Cook as a
kind of folk-hero, East Coast
Canadians have equal reason to
claim the 18th century navigator.
Twenty years before Cook set foot
on the Pacific Coast, he explored
and charted the Nova Scotia, Gaspé
and Labrador coasts. The maps he
made of these regions served for
a hundred years as the standard
guide for mariners, collected in
a volume titled* The North American
Pilot. *Also forgotten are Cook's
role in the capture of Louisbourg,
his raids on French settlements on
the Gulf of St. Lawrence, and his
part in the 1759 seige of Quebec.*

CHAPTER EIGHT

The Beginnings of B.C.

*We should find this a comfortable station
to supply all our wants and to make us
forget the hardships...*

Captain James Cook, 1768

Under furled canvas, the *Tonquin* lay in Clayoquot Sound on the west coast of Vancouver Island. It was a hot, muggy August day in 1811. That summer, strong alliances were at last forming in Europe against Napoleon, and in eastern Canada the militia was drilling against an aggressive United States whose leaders boasted they'd "take the whole continent and ask no favors".

The *Tonquin's* captain, Jonathon Thorn, an ex-naval officer with a bigot's attitude to natives of all foreign lands, had been trading for days with the Nootka for sea otter pelts, worth a small fortune in the Orient. He had sailed northwards from the mouth of the Columbia, where he had landed a group of traders, mostly Nor'Westers from Canada, to build Fort Astoria for the American-owned Pacific Fur Company.

There was already an undercurrent of suspicion and repressed anger among the natives towards men of the tall ships. The Russians trading down from Alaska and the Spanish up from Mexico both had reason to fear the spears of the Tlinkit, Nootka, Haida, Kwakiutl and Salish. Alex MacKay, who had been with Alexander Mackenzie on his overland journey to the Pacific in 1793,

cautioned Captain Thorn about the dangerous mood of the Indians. He explained that they knew little or nothing of European concepts of ownership. But when Thorn saw an elderly Clayoquot chief pilfering, he beat him up and threw him over the ship's rail.

Next morning, crowded canoes were swarming around the ship and MacKay repeated his warning. Once aboard, on some signal, the Indians drew concealed knives and attacked the crew. Thorn and MacKay and about twenty others were stabbed, their bodies thrown overboard. The women waiting in the canoes below finished them off with fish spears. Four sailors managed to fight their way ashore in a lifeboat. The ship's clerk, mortally wounded, crawled below into the powder magazine. The shopping Indians, now masters of the ship, called their fellows from the shoreline to join them in the looting. There were about two hundred aboard when the clerk lit a fuse in the magazine and blew the *Tonquin* sky-high.

This massacre left a stain on the opening chapter of the story of British Columbia. Because of the centuries-old rivalries between the great European powers, the western coast of Canada, a world away from the travelled sea lanes, had only recently become known in any detail. The greater portion of the mountainous interior was still a mystery.

The Pacific Ocean, anything but pacific in

*Il Cap.ᵉ Giacomo Cook
Membro della Reale Società di Londra , e
rinomat.ᵐᵒ per li suoi Viaggi e scoperte .*

One of the most brilliant seamen of the 18th century, James Cook's maps, charts and journals were translated around the world. This frontispiece is from an edition published in Venice, Italy.

**Maquinna
Lord of The Nootka**

When Spanish and British explorers and traders first landed at Nootka Sound, the land they saw belonged to Maquinna, the most powerful of the Nootka chiefs. He treated the Europeans fairly, showing off his wealth and hospitality to Spanish and English alike, and is noted in the diaries of Cook, Vancouver and Meares. In the fur trade, he acted as middle-man, keeping the whites and the Indians honest by taking a "cut off the top" of profits. As a chief he demanded respect, and in 1803, when American traders from the brig *Boston* tried his patience, he captured the ship and killed all but two of the crew, keeping the survivors as slaves for two years. Maquinna's reputation survives in that all Nootka chiefs after him adopted his name as one of rank.

these latitudes, offered no easy passage to the wind ships and conjured rolling banks of fog to conceal its harbours. Nearly twenty years had passed since Wolfe's victory at Quebec, and the American Revolution was in its third year before the first white man set foot on the western shore. He was a British sailor from Captain James Cook's 462-ton *Resolution* who jumped into the shallows of Nootka Sound from a longboat in the late afternoon of March 29, 1778.

a broad inlet of sea

This is the way the official record has it. Doubtless Europeans plied these waters before Captain Cook appeared during his third global voyage, but there is no acceptable evidence to prove that any of them actually set boot to earth.

In the long interim between Francis Drake's 16th century voyaging and the arrival of Cook's expedition, Russian traders had leapfrogged from Siberia to Alaska. From their Mexican and Californian bases, the Spanish colonial governors had made a series of probes into the northern fogs. A Greek pilot, Juan de Fuca, probably desperate to please his Spanish masters, was reported to have found "a broad inlet of sea", and later geographers acted kindly in settling his name on the strait between Vancouver Island and the United States.

Juan Pérez Hernández sailed the *Santiago* in 1774 as far north as the Queen Charlotte Islands but was kept away from the coast by heavy seas.

The British Government had no firm information on these several Spanish voyages when the Admiralty commissioned James Cook, then nearly fifty, to take up Drake's quest for a western entrance to a seaway linking Hudson or Baffin Bay to the Pacific. Cook was instructed to report on "the nature of the soil and the produce thereof; the animals and fowls that inhabit or frequent it; the fishes that are to be found."

Coming up the central Pacific from New Zealand, Cook's two ships, the *Resolution* and the *Discovery*, brought the Hawaiian Islands into the world's knowledge, then made their American landfall near what is now San Francisco. But gale-force westerlies kept Cook well out to sea as he pushed north towards Bering's Strait, and thus he missed both the mouth of the Columbia River and the fifteen mile entrance to De Fuca's strait. When the weather permitted, he closed on the land again above the 49th parallel.

Cook's journal gives us the first accepted description of any part of British Columbia:

The country had a very different appearance to what we had seen before. It was full of high mountains whose summits were covered with snow; but the valleys between them and the land on the coast, high as well as low, were clothed with forest . . . Between two points, the shore forms a large bay in which we hoped to find a good harbour, and events proved that we were not mistaken.

This was Nootka Sound, one of the many inlets and bays of the rugged west coast of Vancouver Island. Cook's description applies today. Very few Europeans of his time had seen anything like that view of range after range of mountains and the unbroken forest dropping steeply to the foaming breakers.

a whole new world

The experienced Cook knew instinctively that there could be no passage east by windship in those latitudes. His navigational knowledge gave him the first true grasp of the immense breadth of the continent. He had spent five years charting the coasts of Newfoundland and Labrador, and he calculated that he was now some four thousand miles west from Cape Race. The vastness of it all, the over-powering scenic grandeur, the lush vegetation, the teeming marine life, gave Cook's men the thrilling sense of opening a whole new world. Some part of that excitement would touch all who followed them.

Among Cook's crew were several who would win renown of their own. One was William Bligh, who became a brilliant admiral but is best remembered for the mutiny aboard his ship, the *Bounty*. Another would soon become woven forever in the Canadian saga – George Vancouver, then nineteen, an ambitious officer cadet.

strangers in a strange land

They all shared Cook's fascination with the local Indians – short, square, heavily muscled men wearing armour of plaited cedar-bark, their bodies daubed with organic dyes. Some sported nose-pins six inches long. Here and there were metal ornaments and implements to prove some contact with other civilizations, but the great majority of the Nookas had never seen a white-skinned man before that day.

These natives, of obvious Mongolian extraction, attracted the anthropological interest of Cook's educated officers. They compared them with the handsome, indolent Polynesians of New Zealand, Tahiti and the Hawaiian Islands.

The Nootkas were led by the massive *tyee*, or chief, Maquinna, who stood in the prow of one of the dugouts wearing a painted mask, shaking a rattle, and shouting some phrases in yet another new language. Cook noted they were "a docile, courteous, good-natured people" and he later named their language Wakashan because of their frequent use of the word Wak'ash – meaning friendship.

Maquinna and Cook became friends and Cook named his anchorage, "Friendly Cove". He presented Maquinna with an engraved broadsword with polished brass hilt. Cook's journal describes the meeting in detail:

In a part of the lavish ceremony to celebrate his daughter's coming of age, the Nootka chief Maquinna supervises the traditional wrestling match that will determine who will become her husband. At the ceremony for his daughter Apenas, Spanish sailors joined the free-for-all.

John Webber, the artist accompanying Cook on his 1778 voyage, sketched this view of a Nootka village. The lodges, over 200 feet long and 60 feet wide, were constructed of cedar planks and posts, some two to three feet in diameter.

Cook candidly recorded his first impressions of the Nootka: "Women are nearly the same size, colour and form with men, from whom it is not easy to distinguish them . . . Though their bodies are always covered in red paint, their faces are often stained black, red or white . . . a disgusting aspect."

All who visited us, men and women, were of small stature. Hardly one of the women, even the younger women, had the least pretensions to being called a beauty. Their faces are rather broad and flat, with high cheekbones and plump cheeks. Their eyes are small, black and devoid of sparkle. In general, they have not a bad shape – except in the legs, which in most of them are crooked.. . .

Their hair is black or dark brown, straight, strong and long. They generally wear it flowing, but some tie it up in a bunch on the crown, and others twist it into large locks and add false hair to it so that their heads look like mops. On special occasions, they sprinkle their hair with white downy feathers from birds . . .

Some men have long beards, while others pluck out all facial hair.

Some of their clothes are made from the skins of land and sea animals, with very little art or trouble. They do no more than form them into a kind of cloak which is tied over the shoulders with a string and reaches as low as the knees. For a head-dress, they have a strong straw hat which is shaped like a flower pot. The men seldom wear anything about their middles and are not ashamed to appear naked, but the women are always decently clothed and appear to be bashful and modest.

Not all of Cook's one hundred and eighty men would have agreed. One petty officer recorded in his diary how, as they gained confidence, the Indians brought girls out to the ships. The going rate for their favours was one tin plate per night. To make them more alluring, the girls were greased with whale oil, their faces painted black, white and red. On the *Resolution*, the jacktars heated a large tub and gave the girls their first bath with soap and water. The diarist added, "Many of us left harbour without a plate to eat from!"

John Meares erected a fort at Nootka Sound in 1788, the first house built by Europeans on the Pacific Coast. The same year he launched the first ship built in the area (using Chinese parts and labour), the North West America *(above).*

**John Meares
The Trader from Calcutta**

Cook had a broad interest in the native peoples and their land. While his ships were fitted with new masts from the magnificent fir available at the shoreline, he examined the inlet, commenting on the intricate wicker-work of the Indian fish weirs, the large communal houses built of split and log cedar, (he entered one that measured 150 feet by thirty feet) and the method of boiling food by dropping heated stones into a wooden trough of water.

The only quadrupeds we saw were a raccoon and an animal like a polecat. But the inhabitants also had the skins of bears, foxes, wolves, wild cats, deer, martens, ermine, squirrels, and of seals and sea beaver [the sea otter]. Among the land birds is a very beautiful hummingbird. Fish seemed to be in plenty . . .

He ordered spruce boughs gathered for the making of "small beer" which they all drank as an antidote to scurvy. He noted water cress, leeks, wild raspberry, gooseberry and currant. He ordered William Anderson, his surgeon, to make notes for an Indian vocabulary.

Captain Charles Clerke, of the *Discovery*, wrote that a girl of three or four years of age was offered for sale with unmistakeable indications that she would be good to eat. A small axe was the price. There are several references in the journals to skulls and skeletal hands being offered for sale.

After a month's stay, his ships caulked and provisioned, Cook was escorted out of the harbour by canoes full of singing natives. After exploring the deep sounds which bite into the Gulf of Alaska, Cook pressed through Bering Strait to Point Barrow, where he was confronted by a twelve-foot wall of ice. Even from the crow's nest, no open water could be seen.

In 1790, John Meares, a British trader operating from Calcutta, single-handedly brought Spain and England to the brink of war over "a spot of ground" located on the west coast of Vancouver Island. Meares first appeared at Nootka Sound in 1786, returning two years later for a new supply of otter pelts. On a third visit in 1789, the Nootka let him build a lodge for his Chinese and Portuguese labourers, and Meares ran up the flag. At the time, the coast was busy with Spanish, Russian and American traders, to whom Meares' lodge meant nothing. It is highly unlikely, too, that Maquinna, the Nootka chief, ever intended to give away the land. When Spanish sailors seized Meares' ships and supposedly tore down the colours, Meares pleaded to the Admiralty. When England threatened Spain with war, the affair was settled.

John Meares' claim of the Pacific Coast was challenged in 1790, when Spaniards captured British ships and hauled down the flag. Britain's naval might forced Spain to back down.

On August 29, Cook reluctantly turned about and took his ships all the way back to "Owhyee," the island paradise where meat and fruit was plentiful and where the bare-breasted girls were as willing as they were beautiful.

There, in a confused melee on the beach at Kealakekua, Cook was killed and dismembered by natives obeying taboo orders from their witch doctors. Midshipman Vancouver played a leading part in securing the return of Cook's body for a Christian burial.

the mandarin market

Captain Clerke took over command of the expedition and made a second unsuccessful attempt to get through the polar ice. He then sailed for England via Siberian and Chinese ports. At Whampoa the otter and other pelts picked up in casual trade sold for as much as seven pounds per skin – some of the British sailors made a year's wages from a few pelts. Fur was high fashion in the palaces of the mandarins.

Reports of this lucrative trade brought dozens of ships crowding into Clayoquot, Nootka, Prince William and the other major harbours. Utter confusion reigned as captains under many flags sometimes collaborated but more often squabbled. British, American, Russian and Spanish interests soon collided.

In the summer of 1786, John Mackay, surgeon of the *Captain Cook* out of Bombay, became the first European to live with the Pacific Coast Indians; he spent the winter at Nootka, under the protection of Maquinna. The following year, Captain Charles Barkley of the *Imperial Eagle* brought out his eighteen-year-old bride, Frances – the first European woman to reach British Columbia's shores. He named two mountains in her honour.

The arrival from India of John Meares, a thirty-year-old ex-officer of the Royal Navy, with the ship *Nootka*, lit the fuse for an international explosion. Meares, an unscrupulous go-getter, was determined to build a land base and corner the fur market. He brought in fifty Chinese labourers to construct a fortified trading post on a plot bought from Maquinna. He launched a forty-ton coastal craft, the *Northwest America*, the first ship built in the region.

In the spring of 1789, while Meares was away with a cargo of furs for China, the Spanish viceroy in Mexico decided to act before it was too late. Esteban José Martinez blew into Nootka full of pompous authority backed by the twenty guns of his warship. He seized several vessels and their contents, demolished Meares's fort and built one of his own with cannons that dominated the anchorage. On June 24, he formally claimed Nootka and all surrounding "seas, rivers, ports, bays, gulfs and archipelagoes" for Spain.

When this news reached Britain, the Spanish action was seen as an unforgivable insult to the flag. Captain Meares soon appeared in London, demanding compensation, (adding complaints of ill-treatment of prisoners). Prime Minister William Pitt, whose father had ordered the attack on Quebec thirty years earlier, now threatened a fight for the other side of Canada. The government voted two million pounds for a war chest, and fourteen ships were put into active service.

a costly insult

The French Revolution was now raging and Spain found itself standing alone against Britain's naval might. Not relishing the contest, Spain agreed on October 28, 1790, to give up claims to exclusive ownership of the Pacific Northwest and to pay compensation. Meares and his association received 210,000 Spanish dollars.

To accept the return of British property and to fill in the blanks on the map of that far distant shore, the Admiralty chose George Vancouver, now thirty-three, experienced by two voyages with James Cook and subsequent service. Vancouver was given two ships, the *Discovery* and the *Chatham*; together they mounted thirty guns with a crew of 154. On April 1, 1791, they sailed from Falmouth, Cornwall, on a round-the-world course that brought them into sight of the North American coastline about one hundred miles north of San Francisco Bay a full year later.

the Columbia passed by

Almost immediately, Vancouver, usually a most painstaking man, made an uncharacteristic error. From the reports of John Meares and earlier Spanish papers, he was expecting to come across the mouth of a large river, perhaps even the "Oregon" of Indian mythology. His lookouts reported a line of breakers where Meare's charts marked Deception Bay. The water had turned from ocean blue to a silty grey.

Vancouver tacked while he decided what to do. Should he send in a longboat to investigate? No, he decided to push on northwards, eager to investigate the Strait of Juan de Fuca. The silt, Captain Vancouver decided, probably came from several small streams joining at the delta.

Just two weeks later, Robert Gray, the American skipper of the *Columbia*, arrived at the same spot. He did send his longboat through the breakers and over the bar, and charted his way some thirty miles into the greatest river of the west, naming it after his ship. That initiative became the enduring foundation of the United States' claim to the Oregon country and eventually the central argument for driving the Canadians back to the 49th parallel in the west.

Followed by Lieutenant William Broughton in the *Chatham*, Vancouver entered De Fuca's strait on the evening of April 29, 1792, believing that no

**John Jewitt
Slave of the Nootka**

On March 22, 1803, Chief Maquinna of the Nootka, massacred all but two of the crew of the trading ship *Boston*. The survivors were a middle-aged Philadelphia sailmaker, John Thompson, and a 20-year-old English blacksmith, John Jewitt. Jewitt was spared because Maquinna wanted him to make weapons; Thompson because Jewitt pretended the older man was his father. The two became slaves of the Nootka chief. For 28 months they lived as the Indians, were forced to eat whale blubber, wear cedar bark robes, paint their faces and in Jewitt's case, marry an Indian girl. Jewitt kept a diary, using a raven's quill and charcoal and blackberry juice as ink. When the pair were rescued in 1805, his journal became a priceless record of a primitive people. Jewitt died in Connecticut in 1821, aged 38.

**George Vancouver
Surveyor of the B.C. Coast**

The son of a customs collector in Norfolk, George Vancouver joined the Royal Navy in 1772 at age 15. He sailed as an able seaman with James Cook on his second voyage, 1772 to 1775, and as a midshipman on Cook's next voyage, 1776 to 1780. Rising through the ranks, Vancouver became a commander in 1790 and was charged with an expedition to take back British possessions usurped by the Spanish in Nootka Sound. His second duty, to explore the shore line, resulted in a remarkable and meticulous survey of the entire coast of what is now British Columbia. Vancouver concluded that he had removed "every doubt and set aside every opinion of a north-west passage" and retired to England. He died at 45, months before his *Journeys* were published.

one before him had penetrated to any extent. Wrong again. After examining Burrard Inlet and Howe Sound in late June, Vancouver "experienced no small degree of mortification" when his boats met up with Spanish captains Galiano and Vales, then busy charting the Gulf of Georgia. The Spaniards informed Vancouver that Captain Bodegay Quadra, the explorer in 1775, now the commander of the Spanish Navy in Mexico, was waiting at Nootka to hand over that territory to Britain.

another oversight

Although he stood on Point Grey looking back towards Point Roberts (he had named both promontories), Vancouver did not perceive the existence between them of the second great river of the region. Fourteen years later, Simon Fraser would reach that delta after his epic down-river journey from the interior.

Vancouver had orders to investigate every indentation of the coastline to give a final answer to the centuries of speculation about an east-west seaway. He set his tars to rowing for days on end as he slowly proceeded up the gulf. Jervis Inlet, and many others, at first held promise of a passage but all petered out into swamps at the foot of the mountains.

In all its probings, Vancouver's expedition got on tolerably well with the numerous Indians, mostly Coast Salish, Kwakiutl and Chinook, and the picture of their life and the natives' knowledge of the white man was sketched more clearly.

Where Quadra's *Sonora* had been attacked by three hundred warriors in 1775, and a boat crew murdered, twenty-seven-year-old Lieutenant Peter Puget of the *Discovery* did his best to make friends. The separate parties of British explorers were always vastly outnumbered and would have been easy victims in any concerted assault. Canoes followed them everywhere, usually at a respectful distance.

When the officers shot crows for fresh meat, the Indians became dangerously excited, crying "Poo Poo" in imitation of the musket noise. Armed with bow and arrow, they menaced a beach campsite, but Puget's courage and diplomacy eased the tension. The southern Indians never attacked the British, but at least one furry "native" opened an offensive. Puget wrote:

An animal called a Skunk was run down by one of the Marines after dark & the intolerable stench it created absolutely awakened us in the Tent. The smell is too bad for a description. This Man's Cloaths were afterwards so offensive that notwithstanding boiling, they still retained the stench of the animal.

At an abandoned Indian village, amid the scatter of islands by Bute Inlet, the explorers walked into clouds of fleas so thick "that the whole party was obliged to quit the rock in great precipitation." Some of the men stripped naked and towed their clothing behind the boats in an effort to get rid of "this troublesome enemy."

a bold stroke

James Johnstone, sailing master of the *Chatham*, made the next bold stroke on the swiftly unfolding map with his discovery in July of the narrow strait that bears his name. The racing tides told him that the open sea must lie somewhere to the northwest and, after following many false leads, he threaded the narrow sixty-mile channel that led to Queen Charlotte Strait. Skirting around the tip of the land on the port side, Johnstone, for the first time, proved the land mass to be an island.

With every onward move, the future British Columbia became more familiar. On August 28, 1792, the Britons entered Nootka Sound, being met by Captain Quadra in his twelve-gun brig,

Activa. Vancouver and Quadra quickly developed a personal friendship, but the Spaniard began to quibble about the extent of the territory to be given up. Both captains decided to check with their home governments. Broughton was sent back to England. On the way he belatedly entered the Columbia and went through a pointless ceremony of annexation.

The diplomatic dance between London and Madrid lasted until 1795 when, again at Nootka, the Union Jack was unfurled as token of British ownership. In a face-saving compromise, both sides agreed to dismantle all permanent buildings, to use Nootka in future as a temporary port-of-call, and to co-operate in keeping other nationals out. With Spanish power waning everywhere, it was in effect a total surrender.

Before he returned to England, Vancouver made two more major forays up the coast as far as Cook's Inlet, removing "every doubt, setting aside every opinion, of a Northwest Passage." Working up the coast from Rivers Inlet, James Johnstone took his cutter into Dean Channel, near what is now Bella Coola, turning at the tidehead where Alexander Mackenzie would emerge from his overland trek just over seven weeks later.

In Alaskan waters, the Tsimshian and Tlinkit tribes proved to be treacherous and aggressive. Two of Vancouver's sailors were wounded by spears and the commander's life was saved by a musket misfire. The war canoes were steered by fierce tattoo'ed old women who exhorted the braves to attack.

In the opening years of the 19th century, the thrusting trader-explorers of the North West Company toiled through the high passes of the Cordillera and raced down the rushing rivers, piecing together a sketch map of the interior. David Thompson finally solved the riddle of the Columbia and floated to the sea where he found the Stars and Stripes waving over Fort Astoria.

During the war for Canadian survival that soon followed, the Union Jack flapped at that remote flagpole, behind the twenty-six guns of HMS *Raccoon* and British authority ran unquestioned from San Francisco Bay to the Gulf of Alaska.

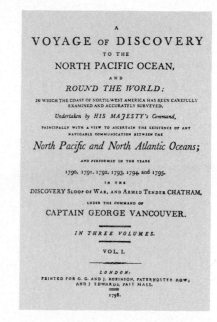

A

VOYAGE of DISCOVERY
TO THE
NORTH PACIFIC OCEAN,
AND
ROUND THE WORLD;
IN WHICH THE COAST OF NORTHWEST AMERICA HAS BEEN CAREFULLY
EXAMINED AND ACCURATELY SURVEYED.

Undertaken by HIS MAJESTY's *Command,*
PRINCIPALLY WITH A VIEW TO ASCERTAIN THE EXISTENCE OF ANY
NAVIGABLE COMMUNICATION BETWEEN THE
North Pacific and North Atlantic Oceans;
AND PERFORMED IN THE YEARS
1790, 1791, 1792, 1793, 1794, and 1795,
IN THE
DISCOVERY SLOOP OF WAR, AND ARMED TENDER CHATHAM,
UNDER THE COMMAND OF
CAPTAIN GEORGE VANCOUVER.

IN THREE VOLUMES.

VOL. I.

LONDON:
PRINTED FOR G. G. AND J. ROBINSON, PATERNOSTER ROW;
AND J. EDWARDS, PALL MALL.
1798.

In the explorer's tradition, George Vancouver wrote a detailed account of his exploits, published in three volumes by his brother, John.

A fiddler saws out the beat for a group of French-Canadians in a circular dance. This old Quebec dance was less rigid than some closely-related English country dances — the Canadiens' version was more of a general frolic. Dances were far and away the most popular entertainment in colonial times, and were sometimes held on frozen lakes and ponds — the travellers wearing skates or moccasins. Some of the gents above wear breeches and others new-fangled trousers.

CHAPTER NINE

They Danced into the Dawn

*I like the parties at the Chateau excessively.
I think it very amusing to walk about the
room and have something to say to everybody
without a long conversation with any.*

Elizabeth Simcoe, 1794

The sound of revelry by night often rose from the scattered forts, towns and cities in the vast emptiness of Canada. Under clusters of candles, the regimental bandsmen kept an elegantly dressed throng dancing, gossiping, tippling and flirting into the dawn. When the 19th century was still young, the long-established social life of Nova Scotia had spread across the Bay of Fundy to Loyalist New Brunswick, to the cities of the St. Lawrence and down the Lake Ontario "Front" to the raw settlements of Kingston, York and Newark.

The formal whirl of balls, dinner and card parties and elaborate picnics was confined almost exclusively to the upper-rank circles of the military and the bureaucracy. As was the way with colonies, they attempted to transplant the exact customs, styles and follies of the old world. In a very different milieu, always a season or two behind the vogue, they went about it all with a hectic determination.

Away from the port cities and the garrison towns – in the intervales of the St. John River valley, amid the Glengarry settlements on the upper St. Lawrence – a simpler, more natural social life

was evolving. It centered on the hamlet, the clearing in the woods, the family cabin, poor and bare as it usually was. A rasping fiddle, wheezing accordion, the twanging jew's harp, just one of these was enough to set boots thumping in a boisterous square dance or reel. Where the forest pressed in on all sides, when the long cruel winters threatened starvation, when armies still marched and burned, the craving for companionship brought people together to "get up" any entertainment they could devise. A man with a fair voice, a Scot with his bagpipes, the Irish clogdancer, found his company eagerly sought.

Among the privileged coterie around Governor James Murray, the bachelor brigadier left to rule Canada in 1760, was the Rev. Dr. John Brooke, chaplain to the garrison. It is to his wife, Frances, herself a parson's daughter, that we owe the best (and almost the only) detailed picture of the Quebec social scene of that day. During five years of her husband's tour of duty, Frances Brooke filled her notebooks with data on the lighter side of life and built this material into the first novel about Canada, *Emily Montague.*

This light-hearted love story, told in letter form, was published in London in 1769. In spinning a romantic tale of complicated courtships, the author (who lived at Sillery) shut her ears to all political rumblings. For her, elections and battles were dull fare. Her liveliest character, Arabella, says:

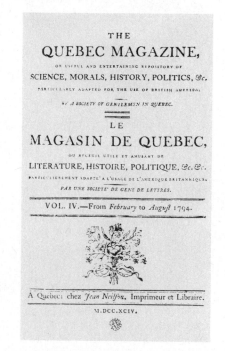

The Quebec Magazine, *published 1792 to 1794 in Quebec City, was the second periodical to appear in British North America. All articles appeared both in English and French.*

**Frances Brooke
Canada's First Novelist**

Periodical readers in London knew her as Mary Singleton, Spinster, editor of *The Old Maid*. But Rev. John Brooke, a parson's son, knew her as Frances Moore, a rector's daughter, and changed her name to his in 1756 when she was 32. Frances Brooke published a book of poetry that year, and when her husband was appointed chaplain of the garrison at Quebec, she stayed behind to see her first novel off the presses. In 1763, Frances joined John and became the first novelist to live and write in Canada. *The History of Emily Montague*, in four volumes, was published in 1769, a year after her return to England. Her high-brow characters were fond of Quebec and society's pleasures, but they found *habitants* "ignorant, lazy, dirty and stupid beyond all belief." In 1770, Frances published her second four-volume novel and continued to write fiction and dramas.

They are squabbling at Quebec, I hear, about I cannot tell what . . . some dregs of old disputes, which have not had time to settle. The politics of Canada are as complex and as difficult as those of the Germanic system.

After a storm piled snow up to her bedroom windows, Arabella comments:

We have amused ourselves within doors, for there is no stirring abroad, with playing at cards, playing at shuttlecock, playing the fool, making love . . . Upon the whole, the week has not been very disagreeable.

When the roads were passable by sleigh, the social round continued with military precision. The governor held an assembly (reception) at the Château St. Louis each Thursday. More quotes from Arabella:

We sweep into the General's assembly with such a train of beaux as draws every eye upon us; the rest of the fellows crowd around us; the misses draw up, blush and flutter their fans . . .

I danced last night till four o'clock in the morning (if you will allow the expression) without being the least fatigued.

An enchanting ball, my dear. We had more than 300 persons, above three-fourths men; all gay and well-dressed; an elegant supper. In short, it was charming.

As the plot unfolds, we get frank insights on the leisurely life – from the feminine point of view – in 18th century Quebec. The ladies practised coquetry as an art, and there is more than a hint that they would occasionally reward their more ardent suitors. "I am half-inclined to marry," Arabella writes. "I am not at all acquainted with the man I have fixed upon; I never spoke to him until last night, nor did he take the least notice of me – but that is nothing. He pleases me better than any man I have seen here." She did marry him, though.

Most of the English upper-classes spoke French and mixed easily with those Canadians whom they considered their equals. Colonel Edward Rivers, who eventually wins Emily Montague's hand, was well aware of the charms of *les Canadiennes*, if he was a trifle rueful:

They are gay, coquet, and sprightly; more gallant than sensible; more flattered by the vanity of inspiring passion than capable of feeling it themselves; and, like their European countrywomen, prefer the outward attentions of unmeaning admiration to the real devotion of the heart. There is not perhaps on earth a race of females who talk so much, or feel so little, of love as the French; the very reverse is in general true of the English: my fair countrywomen seem ashamed of the charming sentiment to which they are indebted for all their power.

Writing to a friend in England, Rivers said: "I prefer Canada to New York for two reasons: it is wilder and the women are handsomer." His comments on Indian women are revealing:

Tis in the bud alone these wild roses are accessible; liberal to profusion of their charms before marriage, they are chastity itself after. The moment they become wives, they give up the very idea of pleasing and turn all their thoughts to the cares of domestic life. They plough the ground, they sow, they reap, whilst the haughty husband amuses himself with hunting, shooting, fishing, all other employments being, according to his idea, unworthy of the dignity of man.

The Indians, to the world-weary English eye, were *"The happiest people on earth; free from all care, they enjoy the present moment, forget the past, and are without solicitude for the future. In the summer, stretch'd on the verdant turf, they sing, they laugh, they play, they relate stories of their ancient heroes to warm the youth to war; in winter, wrap'd in the furs which bounteous nature provides them, they dance, they feast, and despise the rigours of the sea-*

son, *at which the more effeminate Europeans tremble.*"

The English ladies entered in their journals descriptions of the falls of Montmorency, the carrioles and sleighs, styles in dresses and furs, ice fishing, picnicking on the islands in the St. Lawrence, and visits to the many convents and churches of Quebec. Prejudices were admitted without a blush:

I have been making the tour of the three religions this morning . . . I have been at mass, at church and at the presbyterian meeting. The Romish religion is like an over-dressed, tawdry rich citizen's wife; the presbyterian like a rude awkward country girl; the church of England like an elegant well-dressed woman of quality.

But Quebec spun a web of magic for these early Englishmen. "I would rather live at Quebec, take it for all in all, than in any town in England. The manner of living here is uncommonly agreeable, the scenes about us are lovely, and the mode of amusements make us taste those scenes in full perfection."

Chief Justice William Smith, Yale educated, came to Quebec in 1786. He wrote to his wife in New York that "these French folks are the gayest animals on earth."

Irishman Isaac Weld, touring Canada between 1795-97, lapped up the hospitality. The Montrealers, he wrote, "keep up such a constant and friendly intercourse with each other that it seems as if the town were inhabited by one large family."

Describing the gay life of Quebec in winter, Weld said that people met at convivial parties at each other's houses "passing the day with music, dancing, card-playing and every social entertainment that can beguile the time." The taverns in the country at this time were estimated to number six or seven hundred, ranging from log huts to three-storey stone buildings with slate roofs.

The Seige of Quebec *was the feature on this 1792 playbill — sandwiched between farces.*

An Affair of the Heart

A veil of secrecy surrounded one of history's great love affairs, with Canada of the 1790s as a backdrop. *She* was a French baroness with "a hundred names and titles." He was Edward Augustus, the Duke of Kent, son of King George III. Gossips whispered that "the beauties of her mind can only be equalled by that of her person," and they were right. The Prince fell hopelessly in love with Julie St. Laurent, and whisked her (and their baby) off to Gibraltar. When news of their liaison reached the King, he dispatched Edward off to the Colonies, but in no time Julie followed. The two lived openly and happily in Quebec for 27 years and had two sons (five others claimed them as parents). But in 1818, cut off from the Privy Purse and almost bankrupt, Edward bailed himself out and regained his father's favour with a royal marriage. The lovers parted, and it is believed they never saw each other again.

Like most European travellers, Weld was astonished at the ease by which the Canadians got around in the depths of the winter:

By means of carrioles, or sledges, the Canadians transport themselves over the snow from place to place in the most agreeable manner and with a swiftness that appears almost incredible; for with the same horse it is possible to go eighty miles in a day . . . The carrioles glide over the snow with great smoothness, and so little noise do they make that it is necessary to have bells attached to the harness, or a person continually sounding a horn, to guard against accidents.

Prince Edward Augustus, fourth son of George III, commanded the Royal Fusiliers at Quebec from 1791 to 1793, and after service elsewhere, returned to Canada as commander-in-chief, based at Halifax. His romance with Julie St. Laurent (by whom he had two sons) is still one of the world's great love stories.

When Prince Edward booked the whole house for a marionette show in Quebec, the puppeteers, M. and Mme. Marseille, arranged a re-enactment of the American attack on the capital in 1775, illustrating "how the English and the *Canadiens* taught the Americans to live politely with their neighbours." As a finale, the entire marionette royal family (King George was on his horse) paraded across the tiny stage to loyal applause.

When stationed in Halifax, the Prince built a country retreat on Bedford Basin for his pretty French mistress. It had an artificial pond shaped like a heart and the gravel paths, seen from above, spelled out Julie's name.

Haligonian socializing, gargantuan dinners and intemperate imbibing from the well stocked wine cellars of the affluent, was worthy of note to one late-18th century traveller:

Dinner starts at four-thirty or five o'clock and is so prolonged that they hardly ever leave the table before eight or nine. Wines of all kinds cover the table; glass in hand, public and private toasts are drunk unceasingly . . . Then they go into the drawing-room to have tea and coffee, and all this until ten or eleven at night.

Robert Hunter Jr., a young and adventurous London merchant, saw Canadian high spirits on a rather different level. He described the two-week upstream trip by *bateau* from Montreal to Kingston – the route followed by almost all emigrants and visitors to Upper Canada. The St. Lawrence *bateaux* were practical if clumsy craft from thirty to forty feet long with a beam of about seven feet, powered by oars and a lug sail. The voyageurs made thankful use of the small canals dug under the orders of Governor Haldimand to bypass some of the rapids, but usually the boats had to be hauled around the white water after much of the cargo had been unloaded.

The voyageurs entertained the passengers with a boisterous singing that kept their oars in time. The shoreline view was one of dense and silent forest, broken occasionally by a cabin in a lonely clearing, or by the rare village with its rudimentary loading dock. Deer stood to drink without alarm.

The voyageurs made camp at dusk on any suitable bank. Tarpaulins were hung over poles or low branches for shelter, and dry leaves and twigs gathered for mattresses. A bonfire roared. After supper, a man pulled a flute from his pack and everyone danced in the light of the flames:

I never laughed more in my life, many of the fellows who were asleep waked by the noise. They jumped out of bed (or rather off the ground) and joined the dance with all the glee imaginable. Poor devils, they were happy for a moment, and forgot all their cares and difficulties. I footed it away, hornpipe, etc., till I could scarce stand, and then went to bed as hot as fire. I shall never forget it.

When Colonel John Graves Simcoe – with wife Elizabeth and two children – left Quebec at 6:00 A.M. on June 8, 1792, to take up his new post of lieutenant-governor of Upper Canada, three *bateaux* were provided for his party. The gentry sat by day under awnings, admiring the view and accepting the hospitality of squires or petty officials along the route. If the shore accommodation wasn't up to vice-regal standards, the Simcoes used folding camp beds complete with mosquito nets.

While wintering in Quebec City, the twenty-six-year-old Elizabeth Simcoe kept up the diary she had begun before she left Weymouth, England. Very little of social interest escaped her sensitive eye, and she illustrated her pages with informative sketches. For example, she noted the local dogs in harness pulling sleds of firewood and drawing small carrioles driven by children. She ate moose nose, eel and roosters' combs. She attended a concert by the band of the 7th Fusiliers, which was maintained at the private expense of Prince Edward. At a Christmas ball in 1792, she danced with the Prince himself. Col. Simcoe and the Prince formed a friendship that lasted all their lives.

Mrs. Simcoe, although already the mother of six (she left the older children at school in England), loved to dance and entertain. Her diary reports on three nights' dancing out of seven:

Wed. 18th. – *A ball at the Chateau. This being Queen Charlotte's birthday, there were near 300 people.*

Sat. 21st. – *Miss Johnson dined with me, and we went to a dance in the evening at the Fusiliers' mess room – very agreeable.*

Tues. 24th. – *I gave a dance and supper to a dozen of the 7th Fusiliers and as many young dancing ladies. My rooms being small obliged me to invite so few, and only those who danced.*

**Elizabeth Simcoe
The Governor's Wife**

While her husband was embroiled in political, military and engineering matters, Mrs. John Graves Simcoe spent much of her time studying the country and society of Upper Canada. An amateur painter with a keen eye for detail, her diary is packed with notes on social life, cooking, customs of the Indians, herbal remedies and curiosities. When the capital was moved from Newark to Toronto Bay, she turned her attention to the building of the new town, drawing maps and sketching the earliest buildings. Friction between Guy Carleton, the governor-in-chief of Canada, and Simcoe led to their departure in 1796 — a sad day for Elizabeth Simcoe, who had grown fond of the little muddy town that had been their home for almost two years.

Rags and old ropes were the mainstay of the early printing industry in Canada at the time of this ad — used to make paper for newspapers and books. Wood-pulp paper did not come into use until mid-19th century.

Shortly before leaving for Upper Canada, the Simcoes moved into a larger house and, by removing a partition, were able to create a room forty-five feet long, more suitable for dancing. Elizabeth was now able to invite forty to a dance and "I find giving dances much the easiest mode of entertaining company," she wrote. "In this place, dancing is so favourite an amusement that no age seems to exclude people from partaking of it."

the old Château

Stopping off at Montreal on their way west, the Simcoes were put up at Government House – the old Château de Ramezay. Elizabeth admired the size and loftiness of the rooms "which are so much better than any I have been in at Quebec." Joseph Frobisher, one of the founders of the North West Company, had sent his luxury coach to Pointe aux Trembles for their use and he entertained them at his villa, Beaver Hall.

At Kingston, "a small town of about fifty wooden houses" built around Fort Frontenac, Simcoe was sworn in as lieutenant-governor of the province of Upper Canada by the new chief justice, William Osgoode. Hoping to have their town, with its growing naval base, declared as the capital city, Kingstonians tried to dissuade the official party from proceeding farther along the lake to their destination. At the Niagara, they warned, there were few houses and little food and the "certainty of having the ague" – a chill accompanied by fever.

The solid frame buildings known collectively as Navy Hall stood at right angles to the Niagara River close to the water. Here, the Legislative Assembly of Upper Canada met for its first four years, before removal to Toronto Bay. A haughty visitor, the Duc de la Rochefoucauld, scorned Navy Hall as "a small miserable wooden house."

The Simcoes got some elbow room by pitching three tents on the river slopes amid the hardwood trees.

Elizabeth poured tea for the officers' wives of the 5th Foot, encamped by the river overlooking the U.S. border. She entertained ladies from Detroit, relations of the Earl of Mar. She admired raccoons, skunks, a bald eagle and black squirrels which were "as good to eat as a young rabbit." She bought maple sugar from the Indians, and noted that a fishing party of Redcoats took one hundred sturgeon and six hundred whitefish by net in a single day. The sturgeon were each about six feet long.

a great display

That first winter the Niagara hamlet took on the airs of a capital with a fortnightly ball. At one of these, according to Mrs. Simcoe, "there were fourteen couples, a great display of gauze, feathers and velvet, the room lighted by wax candles." Chief Justice Osgoode built his house near Navy Hall and he joined the Simcoes nearly every evening for whist. As the snow swirled outside, someone could often be cajoled into reading aloud from one of the popular books of the day, perhaps Cervantes' *Don Quixote* or Swift's *Gulliver's Travels*.

During all of her four years in Canada, Elizabeth Simcoe never lost her sharp interest in her surroundings or her delight in dancing. The birth of her seventh child (it lived for just over a year) was barely mentioned in her diary.

Before their return to England, the Simcoes moved to York and had a sixty-foot hall erected next to their house, and Mrs. Simcoe threw a ball at which seventy-six persons sat down to supper. Not bad for a log-cabin capital where the attorney-general complained bitterly that he had to cut his own firewood and dig his own potatoes.

Jigs, Reels and Minuets

In an age when courtship and marriage were supervised and arranged by parents, and any kind of contact between unmarrieds was frowned upon, dancing allowed the chance for a casual flirtation. In Quebec, the minuet was the popular dance of the day – an open couples dance of steps, glides and turns. Despite protest from many Protestant churches, in the English colonies, jigs, reels and other country steps made up the repertoire – usually danced to a single fiddler. Bachelor-artist George Heriot must have sat this one out. Titled Minuets of the Canadians, the step shows strong country influence. Note the tambourinist.

Battles of the Great Windships

When border disputes and American aggression touched off war in 1812, some of the most dramatic battles were fought on water. On the Atlantic, the British fleet blockaded American ports, choking off trade with Europe. No match for England's experienced armada, the Americans retaliated by raiding coastal settlements and trading ships. In three years, they captured or sank some 1,600 British vessels, losing about 200 of their own. Off the coast of Boston, the HMS *Shannon* challenged the *Chesapeake* and won after 13 minutes of broadsides. The *Chesapeake* was towed to Halifax and auctioned off. On the Great Lakes Oliver Perry's victory on Lake Erie and the raid on York turned the tide for a time toward the U.S. In August, 1814, British forces sailed into Chesapeake Bay, advanced up the Potomac and burned the newly-built White House. And in September, a naval win for the U.S. ended fighting on Lake Champlain.

The American victory on Lake Erie on September 10, 1813, ended Britain's naval domination of the Lakes, and gave the U.S. command of southwestern U.C.

The defenders outnumbered two to one, the British captured Fort Oswego on May 6, 1814, plundered and pulled down the fort, and drove off the Americans.

October 13, 1812: *The Battle of Queenston Heights. This painting was made years after the invasion and combines the various stages of the battle. General Brock was killed in an attempt to regain the position. Later in the day reinforcements under General Sheaffe forced the Americans to surrender.*

CHAPTER TEN

The War for Survival

... a country defended by free men,
enthusiastically devoted to the cause of
their King and constitution, can never
be conquered.

General Isaac Brock, 1812

There was no question about it. The Americans, spurred by the land-hungry War Hawks of the frontier, were determined to take Canada this time, with no beg-your-pardons. Taking over the remaining British lands on the continent was seen by many as merely unfinished business, left over from the Revolution. With Britain locked into a life-or-death struggle with Napoleon's France, it was the perfect time to strike.

On June 1, 1812, President James Madison asked Congress to declare war on Great Britain. Twelve days later the first U.S. troops headed for the Detroit River boundary. Other forces were concentrated at the Niagara and in the Champlain Pass.

Although control of Canada was the practical aim of the War of 1812, its causes were complex. They included British arrogance on the high seas after the great victory at Trafalgar; the American pioneers' belief that the Indians barring expansion over the Wabash were kept on the warpath by support from Canada; the temptation of the lush Niagara peninsula with its thin population (a third of it from recent American emigration); the stubborn

notion that the Canadians–two-thirds of them French-speaking–would eagerly forsake their distant King if given the chance. From all this mishmash of fact and fiction emerged the stark reality that a rich and aggressive nation of seven-and-a-half million was launching invasion upon a poor neighbour of six hundred thousand. Eventually, the Americans would muster half-a-million armed men.

The odds *against* the survival of Canada seemed impossibly high. In fact, the leaders of the American war party saw it as no contest. President Jefferson had stated that the acquisition of Canada was "a mere matter of marching." Henry Clay, speaker of the House of Representatives and leading War Hawk, said, "I would take the whole continent from them and ask no favors." The Secretary for War, William Eustis, made the silliest call of all: "We can take Canada without soldiers. We have only to send officers into the provinces and the people, disaffected towards their own government, will rally round our standard."

As events quickly proved, the odds were closer to fifty-fifty. The American army of thirty-five thousand looked tough on paper, but it had not fought a serious battle for thirty years and its senior officers were all too old for new campaigns. It was made up mostly of green recruits, often backwoods boys with some slight experience in Indian fighting. The U.S. now consisted of seventeen

POLICE.

WHEREAS authentic intelligence has been received that the Government of the United States of America did, on the 18th instant, declare War against the United Kingdom of Great Britain and Ireland and its dependencies, Notice is hereby given, that all Subjects or Citizens of the said United States, and all persons claiming American Citizenship, are ordered to quit the City of Quebec, on or before TWELVE o'clock at Noon, on WEDNESDAY next, and the District of Quebec on or before 12 o'clock at noon on FRIDAY next, on pain of arrest. ROSS CUTHBERT, C. Q. S. & Inspector of Police.

The Constables of the City of Quebec are ordered to assemble in the Police Office at 10 o'clock to-morrow morning, to receive instructions.

Quebec, 29th June, 1812.

June 18, 1812: *The United States declared war on Great Britain and her colonies. Some days later, all Americans were "ordered to quit the City of Quebec ... on pain of arrest."*

states and six frontier territories, most of them jealous of their rights. This led to squabbling, poor discipline and intractable command problems.

The five thousand British Redcoats in the north, guarding a huge arc from Nova Scotia to Lake Huron, were mostly concentrated in Lower Canada where strategy dictated the heaviest enemy blow should fall. The capture of Montreal would obviously sever the main line of supply and communication, the St. Lawrence, and leave Upper Canada easy prey. But the American mistake in chopping away at the upper branches of the Canadian tree instead of at the trunk was one of the two main factors that saved the colony. The other was the courage, character and dedication of a handful of men–all career officers in the British Army–who inspired resistance to the American take-over, and, through two years of often bitter fighting forced a stand-off which, considering the odds, looked remarkably like a victory.

When the fighting petered out, the British held northern Maine (down to the Penobscot line), Washington had been raided and burned, and, except for a detachment dug in near Amherstburg, not a single American soldier stood on Canadian soil.

a thin red line

Although their lines were thin, the Redcoats were superb soldiers, combat-hardened in two decades of European campaigns. Their cool musketry in the heat of battle, their discipline in the bayonet charge, almost always routed men more used to sniping from the bush. The war was well advanced before intensive training and battle experience produced American battalions able to hold their own in open warfare.

The American lake sailors did rather better, driving the British out of Lake Erie and disputing control of Lake Ontario. Water transport was vital in a country where roads were still few.

August 16, 1812: *According to this notice published in the* Quebec Gazette, *General Brock leading 700 troops and 400 Indians forced the surrender of Hull's army of 2,500.*

At the outset, there was only the 41st Regiment in Upper Canada, but, as luck would have it, the province had passed the previous year under the military and civil leadership of Isaac Brock, a forty-two-year-old professional soldier from the Channel Islands.

heroic destiny

Brock was one of those rare creatures fashioned for heroics. He was six-foot-two inches tall, a blue-eyed blond, equally at home in the saddle and the salon, superbly confident and utterly fearless. He had seen service in the West Indies and the Netherlands, earning a colonelcy at twenty-eight. He had been aboard the flagship *Elephant* at Copenhagen when Horatio Nelson pulled his legendary trick of putting his telescope to his blind eye to avoid acceptance of the signal to stop fighting. Brock too, always believed that attack was the best defence.

When Isaac Brock was a subaltern of twenty-one, a captain in his regiment who had already gunned down several men baited him into a duel. As the injured party, Brock had the choice of weapons. He chose pistols, to be fired not at the usual twelve paces but point-blank across his handkerchief. The other man blanched and protested; in such a duel, both would die. Brock smiled and cocked his piece. The captain blustered, then quit the field in disgrace.

When he took up his appointment at York, with the rank of major-general, Brock immediately set about stiffening defences. There were only fifteen hundred regulars above Montreal, and he knew that Governor-General George Prevost could not then spare him more. In theory, all able-bodied men were on the rolls of the militia, but the government was worried about the loyalty of a large number. And rightly–several hundred actively supported the enemy when invasion began.

Some of them were later hanged for it. On the other hand, districts settled by Loyalists provided battalions eager to have a crack at the old Republican enemy, and some of these units (known as fencibles) were incorporated into the regular army. When the civil authorities in York refused to expedite war measures, Brock dissolved the Assembly and took charge personally.

Brock had been in Canada since 1802 and was well aware that he had little chance of holding the remote western frontier without the active support of the Indians. After the slaughter at Tippecanoe, Tecumseh had pledged the allegiance of his Shawnees to King George III, but the rest of the tribes were low in morale and fearful of the Long Knives, as they called the Americans. A demonstration of British intention and ability to fight was immediately required.

swift and bloodless

As an opener, Brock set Captain Charles Roberts loose from his distant post near Sault Ste. Marie to attack the American garrison at Mackinac Island, guarding the entrance to Lake Michigan.

Roberts had only forty-five Redcoats, but he gathered up one hundred and eighty Canadians (most of them voyageurs) and about four hundred Indians, including Ojibwa, Ottawa, Sioux and Winnebago. Creeping up to the Mackinac cliffs in the early morning darkness, they hoisted a single six-pounder cannon, which was enough to produce the surrender of the sixty American regulars, their seven guns and warehouses full of supplies. The hapless Yanks hadn't even heard about the start of the war.

The whooping Indians, always galvanized by success, now moved towards Fort Dearborn (at the present site of Chicago). When the news about Mackinac reached the east, the evacuation of Dearborn was ordered, but not soon enough. The

August 16, 1812: *American General William Hull hands his sword to Isaac Brock in the ritual surrendering of Detroit. Brock was knighted for the win, Hull sent to prison in Quebec.*

October 13, 1812: *Wounded in a reckless charge to regain Queenston Heights. Isaac Brock lies dying on the battlefield. His last words supposedly were "On brave York Volunteers!"*

local Potawatomis massacred the retreating column, including two women and twelve children.

By then, the amazing Brock had pulled off a much greater coup. On July 12, Brigadier-General William Hull, a stiff-jointed and slow-thinking veteran of Bunker Hill, had led twelve hundred men across the Detroit River. As an invasion, it was a fiasco. He sent out raiding parties to pillage the settlements but never attempted to take Fort Malden at Amherstburg, the only centre of British strength. British scouting parties ambushed Hull's supply trains; a British schooner captured all his orders and campaign plans, and his Ohio militia colonels fought each other rather than the Red-coats. On August 11, the Americans crossed back over the river and holed up behind the palisades of Detroit.

Gambling that the Niagara strip would stay quiet, Brock raced along the north shore of Lake Erie and launched a counter-invasion. On August 16 he led about a thousand men (only three hundred of them regulars) against Fort Detroit. He fired a few salvoes and then sent in a nervy demand for surrender, adding judiciously that his several hundred Indian allies "will be beyond control the moment the contest commences." The demoralized Hull gave in without a fight.

bold and daring knight

In this extraordinary sequence, Brock's boldness and judgment had cleared the entire far west of American strength and gained a mountain of scarce weapons and stores. Detroit yielded thirty-three cannons, twenty-five hundred muskets, ammunition, food, ships, and other transport. Over two thousand prisoners were taken, the 582 regulars (plus General Hull) being marched all the way to Quebec. When news of the victory reached London, a knighthood was gazetted for Brock.

The atmosphere in Upper Canada changed

overnight. Brock's victories rallied the province, the renegades took to the woods, the militiamen dropped their hay rakes and picked up their muskets. The Rev. Michael Smith described the mood:

The people of Canada could scarcely believe the events, even after they were known to be true. The army now became respectable. After this, the people saw that it was as much as their property and lives were worth to disobey orders.

The American assault on Niagara came at Queenston Heights at 3:00 A.M. on October 13. At this spot, halfway between the falls and the lake, the river is only two hundred and fifty yards wide and could be crossed in minutes. From an army of sixty-three hundred, about sixteen hundred were ferried over. They were met by only three hundred men; Brock had a total force of fifteen hundred but they were spread, at the outset, along the length of the river to Fort Erie. A large American assault party under Captain John Wool soon gained the top of the two hundred and fifty foot bluff, capturing one of the few British guns.

final glorious charge

That was the situation when Brock arrived on his grey horse Alfred. He immediately mustered a hundred men and led them in an uphill charge. In the early morning sunshine, he was a resplendent figure in cocked hat, bright red coat with gold epaulettes, snow-white breeches. A sash given him by Tecumseh was around his waist.

In the first charge, an American marksman shot him dead. The attack faltered, and fell back. The Americans seemed to have won the day, and the survival of Canada was immediately in question. But even in death, Brock was victorious.

When he had confirmed that the main blow was falling at Queenston, he had ordered Major-General Roger Sheaffe to bring the Fort George garrison there. The methodical Sheaffe arrived at noon with three hundred sweating Redcoats of the 41st Foot, two hundred and fifty militia and a battery of guns drawn by farm horses. The militia included Captain Robert Runchey's Company of Coloured Men, with about three hundred Indians in support.

Redcoats to the bayonet

Taking a round-about path through the woods, Sheaffe outflanked the Americans on the heights. The skirmishing Indians confused and alarmed the invaders, who turned their backs to the river. One volley from the Brown Bess muskets broke the makeshift line and the Americans ran when the Redcoats came on with the bayonet. Some tried to get back across the Niagara but most surrendered on the cliff top.

The second invasion of the war ended, like the first, in American humiliation. The U.S. forces at Niagara lost three hundred men killed or wounded, and nine hundred and fifty taken prisoner. On the Canadian side, fourteen men were killed and seventy-seven wounded. Sheaffe was awarded a baronetcy for his work but it was the reckless Brock who was to be enshrined in Canadian mythology. He had proved that, against all the odds, Canada could fight and win – and survive.

In 1813, when American eyes did turn to Montreal on the St. Lawrence jugular, the result was much the same: they were easily driven away by inferior numbers of defenders who were boldly and skilfully led. And, in a stirring action on his native soil, Charles Michel d'Irumberry de Salaberry provided Canada with another hero.

The de Salaberrys were one of the several French Canadian families whose sons had been given commissions in the British Army at the instigation of Prince Edward, Duke of Kent. Charles went to war at sixteen and fought in the West In-

Isaac Brock
The Hero of Upper Canada

At 34, Isaac Brock was already a veteran of the British Army when he arrived in Canada in 1803. He was a tall, handsome and easy-going man, fond of reading, riding and socializing. In military matters, however, he was resolute. When he discovered that the garrison at Fort George was about to mutiny and murder the unpopular Colonel Sheaffe, he arrested the conspirators and had seven of them shot. His first concern in Canada was to fortify the small and ill-trained garrison and militia — no easy task. He wrote, "Most of the people have lost all confidence," but added a telling remark — "I however speak loud and look big." At Detroit his bluff won the victory over the U.S. troops (2,500 strong), and he sped to Queenston, where a troop buildup signalled imminent attack. Vastly outnumbered, the general led an impetuous charge to retake the heights, when he was shot dead.

October 5, 1813: *Tecumseh's last stand. The Shawnee chief is shot dead at the Battle of the Thames. In the early days of the war, Tecumseh allied his warriors with the British, and it was largely this added strength to their small numbers that helped the Redcoats hold southwestern Upper Canada.*

dies and in Europe, before returning to Canada as a staff officer in 1810. Two of his brothers died in active service in India, and another in Spain. When "Madison's War" began, Charles was commissioned as colonel to raise the Voltigeurs, a light infantry regiment serving within the regular army. Its troops were to be exclusively Canadians of French descent.

Would *les habitants* fight for Britain? Well, maybe not, but they certainly would fight for Canada. Only greybeards now nursed personal memories of "the Conquest"; their grandsons came forward to fill the companies led by six captains from "the most respectable families in the province." Only men from seventeen to thirty-six were selected, and they had to be at least five-foot-three inches tall. Each volunteer was promised a grant of fifty acres after the war.

soldiers by lottery

Apart from the Voltigeurs, the Assembly of Lower Canada authorized the raising of militia units totalling eight thousand men, to be selected by lottery from the general rolls; those who saw active service were to receive the same pay as the Redcoats. Dr. William Dunlop, later the famous "Tyger Dunlop" of Upper Canada, watched a militia unit marching to the front:

They all had a serviceable, effective appearance. Their capots and trousers of homespun stuff and their tuques were all of the same cut and colour ... They marched merrily to the music of their voyageur songs and as we came along they set up the Indian war whoop, followed by a shout of vive le roi along the whole line.

De Salaberry's Voltigeurs had their great day on October 26, 1813, at a ford on the Châteauguay River, about fifteen miles from its mouth, opposite Lachine. The Americans had decided on a massive two-pronged attack to end the war before Christmas. Major-General James Wilkinson jumped off from Sacket's Harbour with eight thousand men in three hundred boats to follow Lord Amherst's route down the St. Lawrence to Montreal. At the same time, Major-General Wade Hampton, with another four thousand men, moved from Lake Champlain westwards into the heavily wooded Châteauguay Valley, also heading for Montreal.

Voltigeurs' ambush

Hampton, a wealthy Carolina planter in civilian life, expected little opposition. When his leading platoons ran into ambush at a sharp bend in the river (near today's Allan's Corners), an officer shouted for the Canadians to come over to the American side. Colonel de Salaberry jumped on to a stump and shot him.

Although outnumbered by about five to one, the forewarned Canadians had prepared clever defences covering both banks of the river. Hampton ordered fifteen hundred men of the 1st. U.S. Infantry Brigade to outflank the defenders. These troops got hopelessly lost in a night march and at dawn came under heavy fire. Hampton's main body advanced uncertainly down the rough country road towards de Salaberry's front line.

When the flanking brigade was seen to be retreating across the river, the whole army halted, then went into reverse. De Salaberry set all his Indians whooping and his buglers blowing to give the impression of a much larger force. Incredibly, Hampton (who had lost only about one hundred men) retreated all the way back into New York State and took no further part in the war.

General Wilkinson didn't fare much better on the St. Lawrence. Early snows slowed the progress of his convoy, and his regiments were harried front and rear. In one sharp action on John Crysler's farm, at the head of the Long Sault rapids, the

**Tecumseh
The Avenger**

At the close of America's war of independence, many Indian tribes saw the extinction of their way of life "written on the wall." In a final effort to arrest American settlement at the Ohio River, from 1794 to 1811, the Shawnee warrior Tecumseh and his brother, called "The Prophet" (Tenskwatawa), tried to rally the tribes of the old northwest into an alliance against the intruders. However, in 1811, U.S. troops under William Henry Harrison attacked the Shawnee village at Tippecanoe Creek while Tecumseh was absent. His brother was forced to surrender, and the resistance was shattered. Tecumseh joined the British thereafter, and was in part responsible for Brock's victory at Detroit. On October 5, 1813, at Moraviantown, U.C., he was killed at the bloody Battle of the Thames.

**Charles Michel de Salaberry
The Elite Voltigeur**

Charles Michel d'Irumberry de Salaberry (to give him his full name) was born into the purple of Quebec aristocracy — his grandfather was the seigneur of Beauport, his father a member of the Legislative Assembly. The family had little difficulty adapting to the British regime in Canada, and no one in the family returned to France when the option was offered after the fall of Quebec. Like his father, Charles served in the British Army, and while posted overseas, became a close friend of the Duke of Kent. Before he married in 1812, he was one of the most eligible bachelors in Canada. In 1810, he returned to Quebec, and when war broke out two years later, he was commissioned to raise a force of men from among the Quebecois. On October 25, 1813, his 800 Voltigeurs met the Americans at Châteauguay and routed them so handily that the U.S. abandoned the idea of trying to win Montreal.

Americans lost more than four hundred men. Wilkinson had reached Cornwall in worsening weather, when he learned of Hampton's retreat. Sick and dispirited, he promptly abandoned the campaign, burned all his boats and retreated, by stages, back into U.S. territory.

pillaging and burning

As Napoleon suffered defeat after defeat in Europe, the first signs of victory began to show in North America. The British naval blockade of the Atlantic was battened down, and even the most hawkish of the U.S. War Hawks could guess with certainty the next task for Wellington's crack regiments once "Boney" was crushed. Early in 1814, President Madison accepted a British offer to hold peace talks on neutral ground in Ghent, Belgium, but in the meantime, the war continued.

With their control of Lake Erie and their vastly superior manpower, the Americans raided at will along the Canadian shore. Port Dover, Long Point, Ryerse, the Talbot Settlement, the Grand River Valley, all were pillaged or burnt. Only a few scattered detachments of Redcoats and militia could be spared for this exposed territory while the main body of the British forces was split between Kingston and the Niagara forts. The raids could not materially affect the final outcome but they left a legacy of bitter anti-Americanism that would persist for many generations.

Fuming with frustration, Lieutenant-General Gordon Drummond, the new commander-in-chief and head of government of Upper Canada, marked time until he could be sure at which end of Lake Ontario the Americans would next strike. This Canadian-born successor to Isaac Brock had all of Brock's dash and boldness, and before that hot summer was over he would bring the final invasion to a grinding halt in the most violent battle ever fought on Canadian soil.

Commissioned in the British Army at eighteen, Drummond had a meteoric rise. He was made a colonel at twenty-three; a lieutenant-general at forty, and after winning a knighthood for his Canadian victories, he made full general at fifty-five. The wonder is that he lasted so long. Always impatient with delay or defence, he shared Brock's delight in the headlong attack. He was wounded more than once in hand-to-hand combat.

From the moment he reached Kingston on December 5, 1813, the forty-one-year-old Drummond set about reviving fighting spirits dampened by the American success at Moraviantown. In that battle on the Thames River in early October, the faithful Tecumseh had been killed. All the western districts beyond Fort Erie had been abandoned, and the Niagara army had been pushed back to Burlington. Although Wilkinson and Hampton had been baulked in their attempts to reach Montreal, their armies still offered a serious threat to Kingston and the St. Lawrence lifeline.

Newark to the torch

A brilliant night attack at Stoney Creek sent the Americans stumbling back to Fort George on the Niagara, and on December 12, after putting the town of Newark to the torch, they withdrew across the river. The burning of Newark's two hundred houses turned four hundred and fifty women, children and elders into the winter night, and shocked and enraged the whole province.

Drummond hurried to the frontier and ordered an immediate attack on the American shore. On December 18, Lieutenant-Colonel George Murray and five hundred and fifty Redcoats were slipped across the dark river, three miles above the stone-walled Fort Niagara. In a hideous night of flashing steel and screams they swept through the fort; only twenty-nine of the garrison escaped.

October 25, 1813: *The second prong of the American attack – designed to divide and conquer Upper and Lower Canada – was disarmed at Châteauguay (a few miles southwest of Montreal) by British regulars, French-Canadian militiamen and Indians under the command of Charles de Salaberry (opposite page).*

**Laura Secord
Myth or Heroine?**

Whether or not Laura Secord saved the British troops from massacre at Beaver Dam is a question that hardly needs an answer. Historians have no heroes. However, early on the morning of June 23, 1813, the 38-year-old daughter of a Loyalist from Massachusetts trekked almost 20 miles to tell Lieutenant Fitzgibbon of a surprise attack planned by the American forces. When the Yankees attacked, the Canadians were ready and captured about 500 soldiers. Unknown for 40 years, the first mention of Laura Secord was in a magazine published in 1853. And in 1860, eight years before she died at 93, the Prince of Wales sent her an honorarium of £100.

When the success signal boomed out, Major-General Phineas Riall, Drummond's second-in-command, crossed the river with the 41st Foot and marched grimly along the icy border fringe, burning as he went. Lewiston, Fort Schlosser, Black Rock, Manchester (now Niagara Falls, N.Y.) and Buffalo all went up in flames, to the bitter satisfaction of the Canadians watching from the opposite bank.

With Newark avenged and the Niagara frontier cleared, Drummond planned a spectacular dash over the ice of Lake Erie to burn the American warships at Put In Bay. This would probably have returned the lake to British control, but a partial thaw aborted the scheme. Frustrated there, Drummond sent a small expedition from Nottawasaga Bay and Mackinac to retake the outport at Prairie du Chien, controlling the upper Mississippi. He had further dreams of attacking St. Louis.

When the Americans under their new commander-in-chief, Major-General Jacob Brown, decided to try yet again to grab Upper Canada before British reinforcements arrived, General Riall's troops were spread thinly between York, Fort George and Fort Erie. About thirty-five hundred well-trained men – not the green recruits of 1812 – crossed the Niagara near Fort Erie July 3.

every available soldier

When the news reached Riall at Fort George, that impetuous Irishman rushed on horseback to the Chippawa River to check the American advance above the Falls. Riall's troops got a very bloody nose and, by the time Drummond had arrived to take personal command, the invaders had consolidated at Queenston. Every soldier the British authorities could muster was heading by land or water for the frontier.

General Brown waited in vain for naval support, then, worried by Drummond's arrival, he re-tired beyond the Chippawa River. The firebrand Drummond, scenting an opportunity to attack, urged Riall to lunge at the Americans' heels while placing his advance units on high ground where Lundy's Lane joined the road to the Falls, just a mile distant.

Brown's main body, confused by poor intelligence reports, was standing-to at Chippawa, three miles away. As Drummond personally led a thousand Redcoats to join Riall's spearhead, Brown changed plans again and ordered a brigade to re-take Queenston.

bloodiest battle of all

The two armies collided just before sunset on July 25 where Lundy's Lane ran over the crest of a knoll. Three waves of U.S. infantry were hurled back; both General Winfield Scott (later to conquer Mexico and to contest the U.S. presidency) and Riall were wounded. Brown manoeuvred skilfully and his 21st. Regiment crept forward. Then, with a sudden rush, they were over the crest. A third of the defenders were now casualties.

It was the moment of truth for Gordon Drummond. In his dazzling uniform of a lieutenant-general he stopped the rout, rallied his exhausted and dispirited troops, then, sword in hand, he led them back up the slope. Under a thin moon, through a nightmare of glare and gunsmoke, the British and Canadian regulars charged again and again. Muskets and pistols blasted at point-blank range. Drummond was severely wounded, as was Jacob Brown who was also at the heart of the battle.

At midnight the Americans finally fell back, and the knoll was retaken, together with the enemy field guns that had wreaked such havoc.

And that was where the invasion of Canada really ended. It was the bloodiest battle of all: on both sides, 1,386 men were killed or wounded. In the morning, the Canadians found and buried many American bodies, abandoned in the hay-fields and hedges as the Americans hastily withdrew towards their Buffalo base.

There was more fighting, some of it heroic, some of it half-hearted, and all of it pointless. Across the sea, in the gabled city of Ghent, the peace commissioners were languidly shuffling the well-worn diplomatic cards. The peace treaty, signed on Christmas Eve, 1814, sent everybody back to square one. Although Canada held northern Maine – part of the old Acadia – this was given up without compensation by the British commissioners. The plan to guarantee the Indians security in a western state of their own was slipped into a pigeon-hole.

But when the spring of 1815 released Canada from the grip of winter, something new was stirring in the land. From the Bay of Fundy to Lake Superior, and even deeper into the vast Northwest, men came slowly to the realization that the war had not been fought in vain. The big battalions had been beaten back. French and English Canadians had stood shoulder-to-shoulder in defence of their homes and their fields. The border was more than a line on the map. Canada would survive, at least for a time.

This medal, made by the Loyal and Patriotic Society of Upper Canada, was intended as a token of recognition for "extraordinary instances of personal courage and fidelity in defence of the Province." But the award was never given. The war ended in a stalemate, and the list of worthies turned out to be too long for the society's budget.

September 11, 1814: *Britain's thrust into Upper New York came in the closing months of the war. However, after Macdonough's naval victory for the U.S. on Lake Champlain, George Prevost withdrew his land troops into Canada.*

123

Acknowledgements

Just what *was* Canada like during the first fifty years of British rule? While that's not so long ago in the old story of man, it is already a misty time in the minds of present-day Canadians more concerned about what's going to happen next. But we are what we were.

Trying to breathe some life into characters in the national chronicle who are for most merely names in those boring school history books, I turned to the journals, diaries and sometimes ambitious books left by those men and women who actually lived some days of those long-ago years.

Thus, I owe a debt to the soldiers, traders, bureaucrats and tourists who recorded their thoughts and experiences during tours of duty, or just simply during tours. To provide two examples among dozens, I salute Joseph Hadfield and Robert Hunter, young merchant-adventurers from London, who travelled through the Canadas together before the end of the 18th century. Seldom mentioned in academic tomes, they kept their eyes, and their hearts, open.

Dorothy Davies of the Trenton Memorial Library, and Olive Delaney of Corby Library, Belleville, provided the reference works I needed for this book – and I thank them and their co-operative staffs. The volumes of the highly qualified authors of McClelland & Stewart's Centenary History of Canada were consulted, if not ransacked, at every stage.

Leslie Hannon

Photo: N.O. Bonisteel

Leslie F. Hannon was with *Maclean's* magazine for thirteen years; as a writer, managing editor and foreign correspondent. He was editor-in-chief of the *Canadian Illustrated Library* and has acted as executive editor in the preparation of numerous books for several Canadian publishers.

Index

The page numbers in italics refer to illustrations and captions

Picture Credits

Ein Britischer Soldat auf dem Posten, in der Canadischen Winter kleidung. 1766.

F v Germann

kail

From the Battle of Quebec to the end of the War of 1812 in 1815, North America was one of the most active battlegrounds. If at the middle of the 18th century, some Europeans thought of Canada as "just a few acres of snow" not worth keeping, by the early part of the 19 century hundreds of lives and fortunes had been spent in attempts to claim part of it.

We would like to acknowledge the help and co-operation of the directors and staff of the various public institutions and the private firms and individuals who made available paintings, posters, mementoes, collections and albums as well as photographs, and gave us permission to reproduce them. Every effort has been made to identify and credit appropriately the sources of all illustrations used in this book. Any further information will be appreciated and acknowledged in subsequent editions.

The illustrations are listed in the order of their appearance on the page, left to right, top to bottom. Principal sources are credited under their abbreviations:

ROM	Royal Ontario Museum, Toronto
GA	Glenbow-Alberta Institute
NYHS	New-York Historical Society, New York
NMM	National Maritime Museum, London
MTL	Metropolitan Toronto Library
NGC	National Gallery of Canada, Ottawa
WCC-NBM	Webster Canadiana Collection, New Brunswick Museum

1790

Population: 161,311 total.

Colas et Colinette by Joseph Quesnel premieres at Quebec – first drama by Canadian.

Nootka Convention ends Spain's claim in Pacific Northwest.

First sewing machine patented in England.

Russian-American Company claims Pacific Coast north of 55° latitude for fur trade.

1791
Constitutional Act divides Quebec into Upper and Lower Canada.

1792
John Graves Simcoe opens first U.C. legislature at Newark.

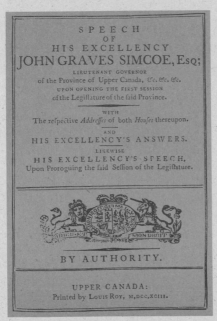

The first bank note issued by the Canada Bank – "five chelins."

J.-A. Panet elected first speaker of Quebec legislature.

George Vancouver charts Pacific Coast and Vancouver Island.

Quebec Magazine published by Samuel Neilson.

Peter Fidler explores South Saskatchewan River for HBC.

1793
Alexander Mackenzie reaches the Pacific at Dean Channel.

Slavery abolished in B.N.A.

Jacob Mountain appointed first Anglican Bishop of Quebec.

Upper Canada Gazette published at Newark – first U.C. newspaper.

American Eli Whitney invents the cotton gin.

U.C. capital moved from Newark to York (Toronto).

1794
Jay Treaty between Britain and U.S. settles Canada-U.S. border.

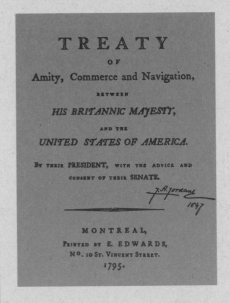

1795
Crop failures lead to embargo against grain exports.

1797
Newfoundland levies 6 pence per gallon tax on rum to pay missionaries' salaries.

Robert Prescott appointed governor of B.N.A.

1798
First canal dug at Sault Ste. Marie.

Richard Coeur de Lion staged in Halifax – first opera in Canada.

1799
Island of St. John renamed Prince Edward Island in honour of Edward, Duke of Kent.

1800

King's College founded at Fredericton, N.B.

Mutiny among garrison at St. John's, Nfld. suppressed – 13 leaders executed.

1801
George Nemiers and Mary London publicly executed at Niagara for poisoning murder of her husband, Bartholomew London.

First issue of *York Gazette* published.

1802
The *Princess Amelia* lost off Sable Island, N.S.

1803
Lord Selkirk's Scottish settlers arrive in P.E.I.

Canada's first pulp and paper mill built near Lachute, L.C.

1804
Quebec Mercury published.

The schooner *Speedy* sinks on Lake Ontario – all lives lost.

American explorers Lewis and Clark reach the Columbia River.

1805
Simon Fraser builds first North West Company post at Fort Macleod.